WRITTEN BY ALISON MALONEY
ILLUSTRATED BY KAREN DONNELLY
EDITED BY SALLY PILKINGTON
DESIGNED BY ZOE QUAYLE

Things TO DO WITH Mum

MICHAEL O'MARA BOOKS LIMITED

First published in Great Britain in 2008 by Michael O'Mara Books Limited, 9 Lion Yard, Tremadoc Road, London SW4 7NQ
www.mombooks.com

A CIP catalogue record for this book is available from the British Library.

ISBN: 978-1-906082-19-2

2 4 6 8 10 9 7 5 3

Printed and bound in England by Clays Ltd, St Ives plc

Papers used by Michael O'Mara Books are natural, recyclable products made from wood grown in sustainable forests. The manufacturing processes conform to the environmental regulations of the country of origin.

Contents

Introduction

'Mum, I'm bored!'

It's a phrase that fills every busy mother with dread. It usually means that she'll end up spending an hour or two playing a tedious board game or will give in and let the children watch yet another video.

But it doesn't have to be like that. Put a little time aside to enjoy each other's company and do something fantastic together instead.

This helpful book is packed with activities for both adults and children to enjoy. Some are practical, some are arty, some are just plain indulgent - but they are all guaranteed to be great fun.

Whether you have ten minutes or a whole day, this book has a perfect pastime for you. Simple instructions mean you can turn your hand to arts and crafts, games, recipes, pampering ideas, magic tricks and much, much more.

There are hand symbols to ensure fingers get chocolatey and muddy but not burnt.

 This symbol indicates tasks that are best for mums to perform.

 This one is for tasks that kids will particularly enjoy.

So go ahead - banish that boredom!

How Does Your Miniature Garden Grow?

Miniature gardens are wonderfully versatile. They can provide a handy windowsill kitchen garden, a tropical jungle for a toy T-rex to roam in, or an enchanted fairy kingdom. You could even recreate the Hanging Gardens of Babylon in miniature.

PREPARATION

The beauty of a miniature garden is that it can be created anywhere. You may have a window box or flowerbed you could use, or you may prefer to use a pot or trough so that you can move your garden wherever you like.

Select your plants. For this you need to decide whether yours is an indoor or an outdoor garden, as this will affect the type of plants that you choose. It is a good idea to ask a member of staff at your local garden centre to help with your selection. They will be able to recommend interesting plants that are suited to your garden's soil and climate. Here are some ideas to get you started.

IDEAS FOR INDOOR PLANTS

- miniature boxwood
- scented miniature cyclamen
- miniature roses
- miniature African violets
- herbs (e.g. parsley)

IDEAS FOR OUTDOOR PLANTS

- alpine trees (e.g. Baggesen's Gold)
and conifers of the
'Chamaecyparis' variety.
- miniature weeping willow
- miniature jasmine
- miniature grass

PLANNING

Next you need to decide how you are going to arrange
your garden. Draw out a garden plan, taking into account
the shape of your plot or container. When drawing your
plan you should add any features you want to include,
such as benches, arches or water features. You should also
mark out where you are going to have any gravel paths or
stepping stones.

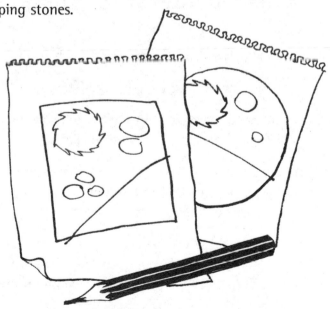

PLANTING

Once you have got your plants and designed your garden, it is time to begin planting.

Place a brick or a flat piece of paving at the bottom of your trough or container. Add some gravel or stones for drainage. Then spread your compost above this about 10 cm deep.

Dig holes in the compost and then carefully remove the plants from their plastic pots. Place the plants in the holes and fill around them with earth, pressing down firmly on the soil. Once all the plants are in place you can add your decorative features (see the suggestions below).

IDEAS FOR GARDEN FEATURES

- Decking – use small pieces of wood, twigs or lollipop sticks

- Patio – use small stones and pebbles

- Mountain ranges – use larger stones

- Paths – coloured gravel for fish tanks work well and can be bought from garden centres or pet shops

- Furniture – you may have dolls' house furniture you could use, but be careful in outdoor gardens as it could be damaged by the weather

- Water features – these can be relaxing places for the tiny inhabitants of your garden or a watering hole for a velociraptor. They can be made from a small mirror or a sunken dish filled with water. Float a leaf and a small flower on this and it will look like a beautiful water lily.

• Glass pebbles – you can buy these at most florists. They make magical additions to the landscape.

UPKEEP

Your miniature garden will need regular watering. Make sure you keep the borders neat, and trim any plants that look like they are becoming unruly. New features like birdbaths or statues can be added as and when you find them or whenever you feel like giving the garden a completely new look.

Delicious Chocolate Chip Muffins

These delicious treats are perfect to make for parties, picnics or presents, or just because they are ever so nice. Eat them warm, not long after they have come out of the oven, when the chocolate chips are still melted and gooey, or if you can manage to resist them, store in an airtight container for another day.

You will need:

- 250 g (9 oz) self-raising flour
- ½ tsp salt • 100 g (4 oz) sugar
- 200 ml milk • one egg
- 85 g (3 oz) butter or margarine
- 85 g (3 oz) chocolate chips
- 12 paper cases

Melt the butter (either in a microwave or in a bowl placed in hot water). Mix the butter, milk and egg in a large bowl.

Combine the flour, salt and sugar in a separate bowl from the wet ingredients. Make a well in the centre with a wooden spoon, and pour the wet liquid into it, mixing together well. Add the chocolate chips and stir.

Spoon the mixture into the paper cases placed either in a muffin tin or on a baking tray. Fill each to about halfway. This mixture should fill a dozen cases.

Place the muffins in an oven and bake at gas mark 6/ 200°C/400°F for 20 minutes or until they have risen and are a lovely golden colour.

Leave the muffins to stand for a few minutes and then remove them from the tin and cool on a wire rack.

Enjoy . . .

Make Your Own Place Mat

Brighten up mealtimes with a personalized place mat of
your own unique design. Make it a family collage or a
work of art, an explosion of colour or a stylish piece of
interior design. Whatever you choose, it beats boring
shop-bought place mats any day. Why not make a set for
the whole family. It'll give everyone something colourful
to look at while waiting for their sausage and mash. Here
are two methods of creating a mat masterpiece.

THE ARTISTIC METHOD

You will need:

- a sheet of paper (A4) • a sheet of corrugated card (A4)
  - paint, crayons or felt tip pens • a glue stick
    - sticky-backed plastic

Get creative. You are now a designer of exclusive place
mats. Draw a picture, a pattern or a series of shapes on
your paper – you could even draw your favourite meal.

When the design is done glue it to the sheet of card
and then cover both sides with the sticky-backed
plastic, being careful to smooth it out (as instructed on
the packaging) so no bubbles are trapped.

Set the table with your new designer place mats and
wait for your dinner to arrive.

THE COLLAGE METHOD

You will need:

- a sheet of paper (A4) • a sheet of corrugated card (A4)
  - collage materials e.g. photos, magazine pictures, foil wrapping paper, stickers, stars, etc.
    - pens • a glue stick • sticky-backed plastic

Choose the pictures you want for the place mat. Family photos look much nicer if they are cut in irregular shapes, rather than square. Glue the pictures to the paper and decorate around them with your other collage materials. Personalize your mat further by writing your name in bold letters.

When the design is done, glue it to the sheet of card and cover both sides with sticky-backed plastic. Alternatively, pop to a shop that can laminate it for you.

Pick-And-Mix Sweets

Home-made sweets make wonderful gifts for friends and family. The bonus in making your own is that you know exactly what goes into them. There are no artificial preservatives, and to colour the sweets you can use natural food colouring, such as beetroot powder, or leave it out.

COCONUT ICE

You will need:

- 350 g (12 oz) desiccated coconut
- 350 g (12 oz) icing sugar
- 400 g (14 oz) tin of condensed milk
- ½ tsp pink food colouring or beetroot powder

Pour the condensed milk into a large bowl. Put the icing sugar into a sieve and tap the side of it with your hand to sift it into the bowl.

Add the coconut and stir. The mixture may be quite stiff so take it in turns to stop your arms from getting sore.

Once the ingredients are mixed together, and there are no dry bits of coconut left behind, line a loaf tin with plastic wrap and spread half of the mixture in the bottom.

Add the colouring to the mixture left in the bowl and stir together until it is an even colour all the way through. Spread the pink mixture on top of the white and then place in the refrigerator overnight to set.

When the mixture has set, remove it from the loaf tin and cut up into slices.

PEPPERMINT CREAMS

You will need:

- 1 egg white • 450 g (16 oz) icing sugar
- ½ tsp peppermint essence or oil of peppermint
- ½ tsp green food colouring or spinach powder

Beat the egg white until it is light and foamy but not stiff.

Sift in the icing sugar and stir together until you have produced a stiff paste. Add the peppermint essence and stir again.

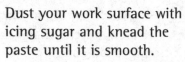

Dust your work surface with icing sugar and knead the paste until it is smooth.

Dust your work surface with a little more sugar and roll out the mixture with a rolling pin until it is a ½ cm thick.

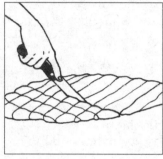

Cut into strips about 2½ cm wide. Cut across the strips diagonally to make little diamond shapes.

Place the diamond shapes onto a sheet of baking parchment and leave them to set in a warm place for 24 hours.

If you can resist eating them immediately, store in an airtight container.

LUXURIOUS CHOCOLATE TRUFFLES

These decadent balls of loveliness are deceptively simple to make and are a great alternative to the obligatory shop-bought chocolates you get at Christmas. Experiment with different essences, jams and liqueurs to create brand new flavours.

You will need:

- 150 g (5 oz) good quality chocolate
- 150 ml (5 fl oz) double cream

- 25 g (1 oz) unsalted butter
- 1 tbsp brandy (optional) • ½ tbsp cocoa powder

Grate the chocolate using a grater.

In a pan, bring the cream and the butter to the boil and then remove from the heat. Stir in the grated chocolate, a bit at a time, until it is all combined and you have a rich, dark chocolatey mix.

Add the brandy and stir. Transfer the mixture to a bowl and leave it to cool and solidify.

Now for the fun part. Once the mixture is solid, use a teaspoon to scoop out blobs of mixture. Roll them between your palms to make little bite-sized balls. The mixture will get sticky as your hands warm up, so dust your hands with cocoa powder from time to time. Place the balls on a baking tray.

Put some cocoa powder onto a plate and roll each of the balls in it until they are evenly covered. Your yummy truffles are now ready to go.

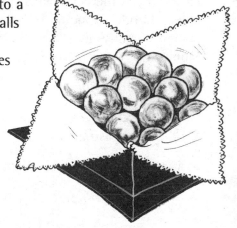

Top tip: Roll your truffles into egg shapes for a delightful Easter gift.

Mind-Reading With Mum

This trick requires two people to be 'in the know' – Mum will be the mind-reader, the other person will be her assistant. So Mum, select a partner and impress the rest of the family with your incredible mind-reading abilities.

The assistant stands in front of the audience, and Mind-reading Mum leaves the room. The assistant asks the members of the audience to choose an object in the room. They then tell the audience that Mind-reading Mum will return to the room and be able to 'read' which item has been chosen. Sure enough, she does.

HOW TO DO IT

In private, before the trick begins, the two performers must choose an item in the room, such as a table, to be their 'anchor' object. The mind-reader knows that the item that the audience selects will be the third thing that the assistant points to after pointing to the anchor.

For example, the performers choose a table as their anchor object. Mind-reading Mum leaves the room and the audience choose the TV as their object. Mind-reading Mum returns and the trick goes as follows:

Assistant: *Is the object I am thinking of the rug on the floor here?*

Mind-reading Mum: *No.*

Assistant: *Is it this table?* (Anchor)

Mind-reading Mum: *No.*

Assistant: *Am I thinking of this chair?* (First)

Mind-reading Mum: *No*

Assistant: *Am I concentrating on this vase?* (Second)

Mind-reading Mum: *No*

Assistant: *Is the object I am thinking of this TV?* (Third)

Mind-reading Mum: *Yes, it is.*

Great magicians develop a slick and witty banter and put on a dramatic and somewhat over-the-top performance. But what they never, ever do is reveal the secret of how their trick is done.

Sew Much Fun

Learning to sew is a great activity to be enjoyed together and means that you will be able to do any number of brilliant, crafty projects. It also means you will never be caught short with a fallen hemline again.

RUNNING STITCH

Running stitch is the most basic of stitches and is used for sewing fabric together. If you master this stitch you can sew almost anything. To secure your stitches begin and end your sewing with a couple of stitches on top of each other.

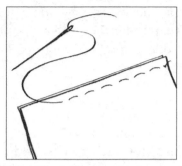

Push a threaded needle through the front side of the fabric. Then push it through from the back, leaving a couple of millimetres' gap. Continue. On each side of the fabric there should be stitches of even length, each separated by the same length of space. For heavier fabrics, stitches should be shorter, and for light fabrics the stitches can be slightly longer.

BACKSTITCH

Backstitch is the strongest sewing technique and will look like a continuous line of stitches, rather like the ones you would get from a sewing machine.

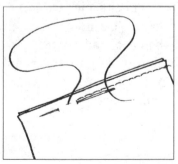

Secure your thread and then do the first stitch as you would for running stitch. As the needle pushes through to the front of the fabric, instead of going forward, bring the needle back to the end of the previous stitch and push through again. Then bring the needle through at the same distance in front of the finished stitch, pulling it back to stitch over the space once more.

HEMSTITCH

This is a clever stitch that you can't see from the front of the fabric. It is great for sewing hems and cuffs.

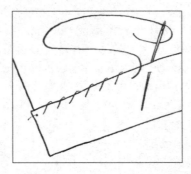

Secure your thread as before, this time sewing your stitches on the spot in the hem and not through the main part of the fabric. Working from right to left, pass the needle through the hem and pick up some strands at the back of the main fabric, just above the hem's edge. Take care not to push the needle all the way through otherwise the stitching will show, then pass the needle back through the hem. Repeat by picking up a few strands of the main fabric with your needle as before.

Make Bird-Cake Bells

Attract feathered friends to your garden with these easy-peasy bird-cake bells. Hang them in a tree and watch as birds flock to these fatty feasts.

You will need:

- birdseed • peanuts • grated cheese • 500 g lard
- string (around 30 cm long) • two yogurt pots (washed)

Before you start, soften the lard by standing it at room temperature for an hour or so.

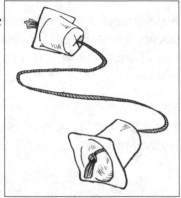

Make a small hole in the bottom of each of your yogurt pots with a skewer or scissors. Thread your string through the two holes and pull far enough to tie a knot on the inside length. Make the knots big enough so as not to slide through the holes.

Cut the lard into small pieces and put it in the mixing bowl. Add half of the seeds, nuts and cheese and knead them into the fat with your fingers. When the mixture is combined add the rest of the ingredients and keep kneading until the lard holds the mixture together.

Squash the mixture into the yogurt pots and place in the fridge to set.

After an hour or so check that the fat has set. Then carefully cut away the yogurt pots. Hang the bird-cake bells over the branch of a tree or from a bird table.

From a discreet distance keep an eye out for feathered visitors and keep a good bird book handy so you can identify your dinner guests as they arrive.

Top tip: Always hang bird-cake bells. Don't let them sit on a bird table or windowsill, as this can attract cats and rats.

Make A Piñata Pig

A piñata is a colourful papier-mâché figure, filled with sweets. It's usually hung from a tree where children can take turns to hit it until the sweets tumble out. It's a brilliant idea for children's celebrations.

Although many people associate the tradition with Mexico it actually began as a Chinese custom and was introduced to the West by the explorer Marco Polo.

You need to allow time for drying, so start making your piñata about a week before the party.

You will need:

- a balloon • 1¼ l water • 40 g plain flour
- newspapers • 5 paper cups, cut in half
- sticky tape • paper for ears
- pink poster paint and brush
- black marker pen • individually wrapped sweets
- strong string (about 2 m)
- a stick for hitting

Blow up a balloon as large as possible.

Tape the bottom halves of four cups onto the body for legs and one to the pointed end of the balloon for the pig's snout.

To make the glue, mix the flour with 225 ml of the water. In a pan, boil 900 ml of water and then stir in the flour mixture. Simmer for two minutes and leave to cool before pouring into a large container.

Tear the newspaper into strips and dunk them one at a time into your glue mix. Run the strip between two fingers to remove extra glue. Smooth the gluey paper over the pig, overlapping them slightly until everything is covered.

Allow this layer to dry before starting another. Aim for three to six layers depending on how easily you'd like the piñata to break.

When it's dry, cut a flap in the back. Burst and remove the balloon and fill the pig with sweets before taping the flap shut.

Paint the pig pink. Cut two ear-shaped pieces out of paper and paint. Then glue them on to the head and draw on the pig's features.

Finally, tie the string around the pig's tummy, then loop the ends over a branch or any convenient spot. Make sure the pig hangs low enough for the smallest visitor to reach.

Everyone should take turns whacking the piñata until it breaks, spilling its contents. You could offer a prize to the piñata champion, but it's probably best to share out the sweets between all contestants.

Start Your Own Slime Factory

Imagine being able to make as much slime as you want. Doesn't that just sound amazing? Perhaps not, but at least it means you will be able to throw out the old stuff that is covered in dust and carpet fluff. Making your own slime is lots of fun, and it means you never need to run out of it again. Bliss.

You will need:

- 3 tbsp borax powder available online or in supermarkets near the detergents
- water • 5 tbsp PVA glue
- 1 tsp food colouring

Mix the borax powder with 275 ml of water in a measuring jug. Stir the mixture until the borax has dissolved and then put it to one side.

In another bowl, mix together the PVA glue, five tablespoons of water and food colouring. Stir until the mixture has completely combined and is an even colour throughout.

Now this is when the magic happens. Very carefully, pour a little of the borax solution into the glue mixture and stir – the slime should immediately thicken. Continue to add the borax mixture a little bit at time, stirring until you end up with a thick, gloopy mixture that you can handle and squash together in your hands.

If your slime still leaves a gluey residue on your hands, hold it under the tap for a few seconds to rinse it off. There you have it, your very own slime to do with what you will.

Top tip: Make your slime last longer by keeping it in an airtight container.

Warning: Slime feels great and is fun to play with, but it is not safe to eat and can be very difficult to get out of hair. Keep out of reach of younger children.

Make A Lavender Bag

These fragrant little bags can be popped in drawers to make clothes smell lovely, or placed in the water for a scented bath. Why not place one under your pillow? Lavender is thought to aid relaxation and sleep.

You will need:

- fine cotton material (muslin or cotton voile are perfect)
- fresh, or pre-dried lavender
- a needle and strong thread • a ribbon
- extra decorations such as embroidered flowers or lace (optional)

If you pick fresh lavender, place the stems on a wire rack until completely dry. Then transfer them into a paper bag in a warm place, such as an airing cupboard. If possible, space the stems out so they are not touching. Leave the lavender for about a week and then strip the flower heads from the stems.

While waiting for the lavender to dry, cut the cotton material into two squares measuring 15 cm by 15 cm.

With the front of the two panels facing each other, stitch around three sides of the square using backstitch (see page 23). Leave the top side open.

Fold over a small hem of 1½ cm at the top and neatly sew using hemstitch (see page 24). Turn your bag the right side out and sew on any extra decorations you would like to add.

Fill the bag with lavender. Then, using a loose running stitch (see page 22), sew up the final side 2½ cm from the top of the bag. As you stitch, pull the thread taut to produce a gathered look.

When you have finished stitching, pull the thread taut once more and tie off.

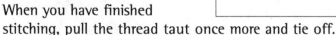

Add a ribbon around the gathered top of your bag and tie into a bow.

Create A Modern Masterpiece

BEAUTIFUL BLOW PICTURES

Blow painting makes really interesting pictures. It is particularly good for creating tree scenes.

You will need:

• paper • drinking straws • runny, water-based paint

Dilute the paint until it is runny then put a few drops onto the paper. For trees, put the drops of paint at the

bottom of the page. Using the straw, blow the paint until you have achieved a pattern you like.

Turn the paper around and repeat with a different colour. Whatever you do, remember you have to blow, not suck. Keep going with more colours, until the picture is complete, and then leave to dry.

PAINTING WITH MARBLES

Paint-covered marbles will make great patterns on a plain sheet of paper, but be warned, it can get messy.

You will need:

- a washing up bowl or deep tray
- different coloured craft paints in small pots
- white paper • a few marbles • plastic spoons

Cut the paper to fit into the base of the bowl or tray and place it at the bottom.

Coat a marble with paint by dropping it into one of the paint-filled containers. Lift it out using a spoon and drop it onto the paper. Tilt the bowl or tray in different directions so the marble leaves a colourful trail.

Repeat with different coloured paints until you have a pattern all over the paper. When the picture is finished remove from the bowl and leave to dry.

How To Customize A T-Shirt

Calling all hippy chicks and surfer dudes – if you have an old white T-shirt that you never wear, here are two great ways to give it a new, seriously cool, lease of life.

TIE-DYE

A tie-dyed T-shirt is eye-catching but simple to achieve.

You will need:

- a white or light-coloured cotton T-shirt or top
- a bowl (bear in mind you won't be able to use it for food again) • rubber bands or pieces of string
- rubber gloves • a bucket
- cold-water dye and cold dye fix
- an old towel or tea towel
- an old wooden spoon or wooden washing tongs
- cold water • hot water • 6 tbsp salt

Plan your design. For example, do you want small patterns in one area, or large circles all over? You can even have stripes. Look at the different items on pages 38 and 39.

Dampen the T-shirt by submerging it in water, then squeeze out the excess. If it is a new top wash it first.

To create tie-dye circles, gather large or small bunches of fabric and twist rubber bands or tie the pieces of string tightly around the bottom of each bunch.

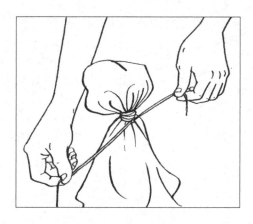

Put the bucket in the sink or bath and pour in two litres of cold water. Pour half a litre of hot water into a bowl and mix in the dye. Pour the dye mixture into the bucket and wash the bowl. Pour another half a litre of hot water into the bowl and mix it with the dye fix and the salt. Stir until all of the salt has dissolved and then pour the mixture into the bucket. Wearing rubber gloves, submerge the T-shirt into the diluted dye and stir slowly with the spoon or tongs for ten minutes. Poke the cloth to keep it submerged.

Leave the T-shirt in the bucket for an hour, stirring occasionally. Take out and rinse under cold water until the water runs clear.

Squeeze the shirt and then roll it in the towel or tea towel to remove excess water. Now take off the bands and marvel at the cool tie-dye effect.

Top tip: You may be eager to try out your new look but you have to wash and dry the T-shirt first. You don't want to end up with green skin!

DIFFERENT PATTERNS

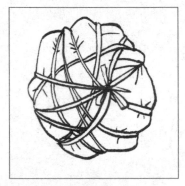

Marble Effect. For an all-over marbled effect, scrunch up the T-shirt and tie string or fasten rubber bands around it in a random fashion before dying.

Concentric Circles. For concentric circles (circles within circles) pinch a spot of fabric and then use several rubber bands spaced at regular intervals along the the length of the fabric. You can do one big 'bullseye' pattern or a few smaller ones by using as many bands as you like.

Sunburst. Use marbles to create a different effect. For a sunburst pattern, wrap some material around a marble and then fix several rubber bands around the bunched fabric below, a centimetre or so apart.

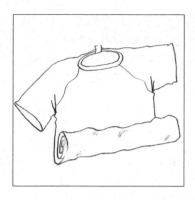

Stripes. For stripes, roll your T-shirt from top to bottom like a sausage as shown. Then place the rubber bands at intervals along the material.

BATIK T-SHIRT

Batik is thought to date back more than 2,000 years, but its exact origins are unknown. Batik is most common in Java and Bali, in Indonesia, where it was once the mark of wealth, position and even royalty.

Traditionally, designs are achieved with the use of hot wax, but to keep creative fingers from burning, here is a safer alternative. However, you will need patience – and a few days to spare.

You will need:

- white or light-coloured cotton T-shirt
- 75 g (2¾ oz) flour • 115 ml water
- 1 sheet of thick paper • cold-water dye • a paintbrush
- an old washing-up liquid or squeezy bottle
- 1 sheet of cardboard (the side of a cereal box will do)

First plan your design. Try it on rough paper first, colouring it in to see what the T-shirt will look like. Remember to think about colour – if you are painting red dye on to a yellow T-shirt, for example, it may look orange.

Cut the paper to the shape and size you want the design to be (e.g. square or circular). Sketch your design on to the paper, then cut it into a stencil. The flour paste needs to go into the holes so don't make your design too fiddly or it will be difficult to cut out.

Mix the flour and water together. Pour the mixture into the squeezy bottle and replace the lid. Slot the cardboard between the front and back of the T-shirt to protect the fabric behind your design.

Lay the stencil on to the front of the T-shirt and carefully squeeze the flour paste into the holes. The areas covered in glue will be the ones that stay the same colour as the T-shirt. Now squeeze the paste around the edge of the stencil – this will stop the dye running out of the border.

Carefully remove the stencil and leave the mixture to dry – this can take up to two days, so be patient.

When the T-shirt is completely dry, mix up some cold-water dye according to the instructions on the pack.

Paint over your design using the brush. Be careful not to leave any gaps and not to go outside the border of your design. Leave the T-shirt to dry for another day.

When your design is completely dry, carefully peel off the paste and wash the T-shirt. At last, you can wear your unique T-shirt with pride.

Animal Magic With Cards

If you like 'Snap' you will love this card game with some extra animal chaos thrown in. The object of the game is to be the player left with all the cards.

You will need:

• a pack of cards • pen and paper • a bowl

Each player chooses an animal and writes it down on a scrap of paper. The animals' names should be as long or hard to say as possible, such as gnu or hippopotamus. Put the pieces of paper in the bowl and each player then picks one out and shows it to everyone else.

The cards are then dealt into piles, face down until the pack is gone. Players are not allowed to look at their cards.

The player to the left of the dealer turns their top card over to start a face-up pile. The other players do the same, one by one. This continues until a player spots that another player has a card with the same number or picture as their own. They must then shout out the name of the other player's animal three times.

If a player shouts out the correct animal and in a way that doesn't mangle the name, they win the other player's face-up pile. If they get it wrong they must give up their own face-up pile to the other player.

The winner is the player left with all the cards.

Deck The Halls With Homemade Garlands

Have a green Christmas with seasonal garlands made from rubbish and popcorn strings that the birds will enjoy when your festivities are over.

POPCORN STRINGS

Traditionally, strings of popcorn are used as decorations in the United States, where they have been hung on Christmas trees since the 19th century. As many an American bird knows, however, they also make excellent bird feeders when hung from a branch outside.

You will need:

- popping corn • a microwave or saucepan with lid
  - a needle with a large eye
  - strong thread or dental floss (unminted)

 Pop lots of corn according to the packet instructions, especially if you want to eat some yourself, but remember to leave some for your feathered friends! Put aside to cool.

Cut your cotton or floss to double the length you want your popcorn string to be, and thread it through the eye of the needle until the two ends are level. Tie a large knot at the end of the strands then, if your corn is cool enough, push the needle through the centre of the first piece.

Make sure the knot at the bottom is big enough to hold the popcorn on and then thread the popcorn on one at a time.

Continue until the string is almost full with a gap of 5 cm at the top. Then cut the thread to remove the needle and tie the loose ends into a knot.

Popcorn strings can go on your Christmas tree or decorate your mantlepiece. After Christmas use the thread at the top to tie the strings to a tree and give the birds a festive feast.

If you don't want to pop your own corn, you can use shop-bought but please steer clear of the salted variety. Plain is best for the birds.

Top tip: Cranberries and blueberries also make an attractive and tasty addition to your popcorn strings.

GARLANDS OF PAPER BEADS

Transform rubbish into bright and colourful garlands that are very easy to make. The best bit is that you can find all the things you need about the house so it helps with the recycling.

You will need:

• strong thread or elastic • drinking straws
• old magazines • pen • ruler • threadable bits
and bobs – old buttons, beads, keys etc • scissors
• paints and brushes • PVA or craft glue

To make the beads cut out lots of long triangles from a magazine. Make the base of each triangle as wide as you want the beads to be on your garland. Long triangles will make the beads thicker and shorter triangles will make them thin – a variety looks great.

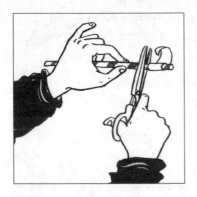

Next, cut lengths of straw the same length as the bases of your triangles. Then glue the base of each paper triangle to a straw section.

Wrap the rest of the triangle round the straw until you reach the tip. Glue the tip into place.

When the beads are dry, paint them in bright colours. Metallic paints can look great too, or they may look cool just as they are, in which case seal them with a coat of PVA glue.

Cut the thread or elastic to the length you want the garland, leaving a little extra for tying a knot. Thread on your beads, putting your buttons, keys, etc. at intervals along the string.

The Shopping List Game

This game is a great test of memory. Players work their way through the alphabet, taking it in turns to complete the sentence '*I went shopping and I bought ...*'

The first player might say: '*I went shopping and I bought an apple.*'

The next player would then repeat this sentence, adding an item begining with b.

For example: '*I went shopping and I bought an apple, and a basketball.*'

Keep taking it in turns, repeating the sentence and the list of items that have been bought so far, and adding another item to the end of the list.

If someone forgets an item, lists the items in the wrong order, or pauses for longer than a count of five, they are out. The winner is the person who stays in the game the longest.

Top tip: This game can also be played with the sentence '*I am going to a party and I am going to bring ...*'

A Spa Day Treat For Mum

When Mothers' Day or Mum's birthday comes around, what could be more special than creating her own personal health spa at home? There's no need to spend money on expensive skin-care products – you can make your own from the contents of the kitchen cupboard and fridge.

Put on Mum's favourite CD of relaxing music and tell her to wrap up in her dressing gown. It's time for her to relax.

Warning: If Mum can't eat any of the following ingredients, because of an allergy, don't spread it on her skin!

OATMEAL AND HONEY FACEPACK

You will need:

- 75 g (2¾ oz) oatmeal • 3 tbsp honey • 1 egg yolk

Crack an egg over a bowl, keeping the yolk in one half of the shell. Pass the yolk from one half of the shell to the other, letting the white slip into the bowl below. When the shell contains just the yolk, tip this into another bowl and save the white to use for something else.

Add the rest of the ingredients to the egg yolk and stir until they are thoroughly mixed.

Use a paintbrush to apply the mixture to Mum's skin,

using circular movements. Be careful to avoid the eye area. Then tell Mum to sit back and relax for ten minutes. When the time is up, rinse off the facepack with warm water or cool rose water.

BANANA AND HONEY FACEPACK

Use a fork to mash a ripe banana. Add a teaspoonful of honey and mix together well.

STRAWBERRY FACEPACK

Mash four large strawberries and spread the pulp onto the skin.

COOLING CUCUMBER AND YOGURT FACEPACK

Purée a quarter of a cucumber in a blender and mix with a tablespoonful of plain yogurt – the sweetened fruit variety really doesn't work for this.

OLIVE OIL AND OATMEAL SCRUB

You will need:

- 2 tbsp ground uncooked oatmeal
- 1 tbsp olive oil • 1 tbsp lemon juice
- 1 tbsp brown sugar • 1 tsp of honey

Mix the ingredients together in a bowl and apply to Mum's face with firm circular movements. Rinse off with warm water.

AVOCADO AND BANANA SCRUB

You will need:

- 1 dried avocado stone (left to dry for three days or more beforehand) • ½ ripe banana
- 1 tbsp olive oil • plastic bag and hammer

Place the avocado stone into a plastic bag (make sure it has no holes), then smash with a hammer until the pieces are fine. Mash the banana and mix it with the pit powder and olive oil. Apply with firm circular movements. Rinse off with warm water.

Top tip: After all these treatments, Mum should splash her face with cold water to close the pores, and then pat dry with a clean towel.

Make A Dream Catcher Mobile

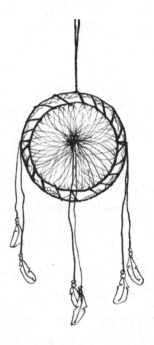

Native Americans believed that dreams travelled through the air before reaching sleepers. They hung dream catchers up to stop bad dreams from coming their way. The nightmares got caught in the webs, while the good dreams slid off the feathers at the bottom and dropped softly on to the sleepers below.

You will need:

- a netting fruit bag • coloured wool
- a round plastic lid from an ice cream container

• beads • coloured feathers (available at craft shops and some supermarkets) • scissors • craft glue • a hairgrip

Cut out the middle of the ice cream container lid, leaving the plastic rim. This can be done with scissors but it might be easier with a craft knife.

Pull the netting tightly over the rim, then tie together at the back.

Using the hairgrip as a needle, wind the wool tightly round the outside of the hoop and through the mesh until the rim is covered. Then tie the ends of the wool together. Tie a loop of wool to the top of the hoop to hang it up.

Cut away the rough ends of the netting at the back of your dream catcher using scissors.

Cut three strands of wool, about 60 cm long, for the beads. Double the strands over and tie the folded ends to the sides and middle of the dream catcher. Make sure the loose ends hang down. Then add your beads. Tie a large knot in the wool to keep the beads on.

Now glue a feather to the bottom of each strand.

The dream catcher needs to be suspended within a few feet of the bed and able to move freely. If possible, it is best to hang it from the ceiling. Sweet dreams!

Grow Froggy Friends

Collecting frogspawn and rearing tiny black tadpoles until they are little jumping froglets is a fascinating springtime activity that brings the magic of nature into your home.

You will need:

- a fishing net • a bucket
- a fish tank with a lid • fish food flakes

Start checking local ponds for frogspawn in early spring. When you find a pond with lots of spawn, use a net to scoop out a small isolated clump. Be careful not to break up a large clump or the delicate eggs inside could get damaged.

Transfer the frogspawn into a bucket filled with water from the pond. Add some pondweed. The young tadpoles will eat this as they grow, and it will help to oxygenate the water.

Fill the fish tank with tapwater and de-chlorinate it by leaving it outside for a few days to settle. Alternatively, use a chemical bought from a local pet shop. Follow the instructions on the packaging. It is important to do this because tap water contains chemicals that can kill tadpoles.

Carefully transfer the frogspawn and pondweed to the tank. Now you have to wait patiently for the wiggling tadpoles to emerge.

Watch the frogspawn closely as the days pass. The small black dots will grow larger and elongate as the tadpoles grow inside the eggs. When they emerge the new tiny tadpoles are not very exciting at first. They do not eat and stay very close to the clump of spawn getting their nutrients from their empty egg.

As they get larger they will move about more and begin to feed on the weed taken from their home pond. Eventually they will sprout gills at the sides of their heads to get oxygen from the water, and their bodies will fatten.

After about a week or so, front legs will begin to grow and the tadpoles will begin to crave a more meaty diet. Fish food flakes are good for this, but be careful not to add too many or the water will get very dirty. Adding a bit more pond water at this stage will also give them a little natural food.

As their tails shrink and their back legs begin to grow the tadpoles will want to get out on land. Put a rock in the tank so that they are able to climb out above water level and breathe with their newly developed lungs. Note that their gills have completely disappeared.

Put a lid on your tank so your frogs don't escape. Now the frogs are on the move it is time to set them free.

Take your little froglets back to the pond they came from, or they will be hopping mad.

Great Avocado Ghouls

These tasty, nutritious treats look pretty scary, and are ideal for Halloween. They might look frightening, but they taste heavenly enough for any day of the year.

You will need:

- 2 ripe avocados • a 185 g can of tuna
- ½ a lemon • 8 capers
- fresh parsley • 4 pitted black olives
- 1 tomato

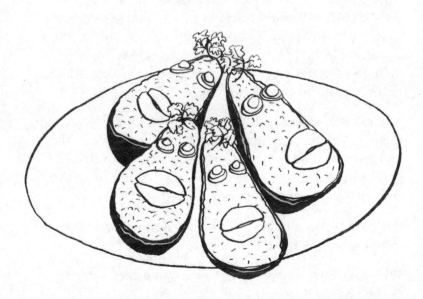

Cut the avocados in half and remove the stones. Scrape the flesh into a large bowl, without damaging the skin. Squeeze the juice of half a lemon into the bowl with the avocado flesh. This will make your ghouls taste nice and also stop the flesh from turning brown.

Drain the can of tuna, then add it to the mixture in the bowl. Mash together until thoroughly mixed and then spoon into the empty avocado cases. Press down until the tops are smooth.

Cut the olives in half and place two pieces on each avocado half for eyes. Add a caper to each eye as a pupil. Slice the tomato and use half a slice to make each ghoul's gruesome smile.

For an easy vegetarian version of this dish, leave out the tuna and mix in some finely chopped tomatoes instead, to make a guacamole filling.

Top tip: Ghouls can come in many shapes and delicious disguises. Why not create your own terrifying taste sensations? You could use small chunks of pepper for scary red eyes or bits of radish for horrid fangs.

Have A Freaky Friday

Freaky Friday is a classic movie that sees Tess Coleman, a stylish single mother (played by Jamie Lee Curtis) and her rock chick daughter Ana Coleman (Lindsay Lohan) switch places for a whole day. If you haven't seen this film, then watching it is a great 'thing to do with Mum'.

What would it be like to switch places in real life? What if Mum suddenly had to do homework again or go to bed at a certain time? Or what if the kids were in charge, and could decide what was for dinner or how much TV they were allowed to watch?

Have your own Freaky Friday, Thursday, Sunday or any other day and find out.

THE SWAP

Mum, take a look through your wardrobe and see what outfits are most like something a child would wear. Loud T-shirts and jeans are best for this. Jeans should be rolled up to give a more youthful look. Or you could try and fashion some kind of school uniform. Take special care to adopt any peculiarities of your child's speech, such as using two syllables to say mum – 'Oh Muu-um!'

Kids, think about how Mum speaks. If she has any embarrassing pet names for you, such as Mugwump or Fanny Fennakapan, you can now call her these names for the whole game and see how much she likes it.

THE GAME

There are no rules for this game apart from acting like each other. Let your imaginations run riot. Mum may not want to do homework when she is told to and may go and switch on the TV. Kids may want the family to have Swiss roll and baked beans for dinner.

Make sure you remember to swap back again before the school-run or you could get some very strange looks.

Make A Spectacular Firework Display Picture

Firework displays can be great fun, but it can be tricky to take a really good photograph of fireworks – because blink and you will miss them. With these pictures you can get inspiration from your next local display and then come home and make some spectacular displays of your own.

You will need:

- a sheet of paper • colouring pens or pencils
- a large black wax crayon • a pen lid or small coin

Put some sheets of newspaper down to protect the surface you're working on. Now take the coloured pens and start tackling the big, white space of the paper. You want to cover the whole sheet in colour – so get stuck in. Try rainbow stripes, random blobs, connecting squares, or anything you like. Just make sure that every bit of white is covered with all of your favourite colours.

When your paper is covered in colour take your black crayon and scribble over your page until it is all black. Don't hold back, the blacker the better. Remember this is supposed to be the night sky.

When the page is completely covered in black crayon and none of the colours underneath are visible you're ready to 'draw' your picture. Use a small coin or the lid of a pen to scratch into the surface of the black crayon and reveal the bright colours beneath. Add swirls, star-bursts and spirals, dots, rocket shapes and sparklers. Spectacular!

The great thing is, if you make a mistake or you get bored of your picture, just grab your black crayon again, cover the picture up and start again.

Make Petal Perfume

Kylie has one, J-Lo has one – how about creating your own signature scent? Girls can wear it and boys can give it as a gift (remember some of the greatest perfumers in the world are male). Hunting for the petals for your very own perfume is the perfect way to while away a long hot summers' day. Decide together which flowers to use, to avoid destroying Dad's prize-winning dahlias.

CLASSIC ROSE PERFUME

Classic Rose Perfume will smell wonderful for a few days but can go off quite quickly. Storing it in the fridge will make it last longer and very refreshing to apply.

You will need:

- rose petals – as many as you can find

- 2 clean jars • an attractive glass bottle or scent bottle • a strainer • water

Put the petals into the jar and add enough water to cover them and then about 1 cm more. Leave in a warm sunny spot for at least a day.

Wash the scent bottle with warm water and washing-up liquid, then rinse with a solution of water and a few drops of white vinegar. Be careful not to add too much or your perfume could end up smelling like a bag of chips!

Strain the petal water into a clean jar, squashing the petals to extract more scent. Pour into the nice, clean bottle.

HEAVENLY BLOSSOM SCENT

This recipe will work well with any fragrant blossoms, but look out for lavender, honeysuckle and lilac as these are particularly good. This scent also has the advantage of keeping longer and will stay fresh for up to a month.

You will need:

- 2 cups water • 1 cup chopped petals or flowers
- 1 muslin or pudding cloth • a bowl
- white vinegar • a glass bottle

Lay the muslin in the bottom of the bowl so that the edges come over the side. Place the petals into the bowl and add water until the petals are completely submerged. Cover the bowl and leave overnight.

The following day, carefully lift the muslin out of the bowl, drawing the corners in to avoid dropping the petals. Gather up the corners and squeeze the water out of the muslin into a small clean saucepan, adding any water left in the bowl.

Bring to the boil and simmer until a small amount of liquid (about a tablespoonful) is left, then remove from the heat and leave to cool.

Pour your scent into the bottle and add a pretty ribbon.

Rustle Up A Leafy Autumn Scene

The vibrant reds, browns and yellows of autumn leaves make woods and gardens look beautiful and can also make a stunning work of art.

Choose a crisp, blue-skied autumn day and go out for a long walk. Leaves can be found just about anywhere there are trees and nobody minds if you pick them up off the ground. Make sure you dust off any bugs before you put them in your bag.

Collect as many different shapes and colours as you can.

PRESERVING LEAVES

You will need:

• a variety of autumn leaves • wax paper • acrylic craft spray from a craft shop • an iron

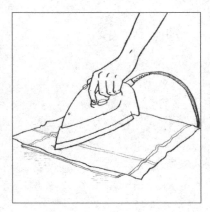

Place the leaves between two layers of wax paper and cover with an old towel or piece of cloth.

Iron the fabric with the iron on a warm setting. This will seal the sheets of wax paper together with the leaf in between.

Cut around the shape of your leaf, leaving a narrow margin of wax paper around the leaf edge.

Set aside your leaves for a day or two and then spray them with a sealant, such as acrylic craft spray.

PRESSING LEAVES

If you can't find any wax paper, don't despair. You can still make a marvellous picture by pressing the leaves between the pages of a large book.

You will need:

- a variety of autumn leaves • some sheets of newspaper
- a large heavy book • some other books to rest on top

Place each leaf between two sheets of newspaper and press between the pages of the large book.

Leave at least a ½ cm of book pages between each leaf you press. When the book is full of leaves, shut it and place more books on top for extra pressure.

Leave these for about two weeks and then remove each leaf carefully.

THE PICTURE

When the leaves are ready, you can create a picture. Take a sheet of paper and experiment with where to position the leaves. Some leaves make great fish shapes. When you are happy with your design, stick the leaves down with PVA glue and leave to dry.

Perfect A Picnic Pan Bagna

Pan Bagna literally means 'bathed bread' as the bread is bathed in dressing so that it absorbs all the delicious flavours from the filling.

Pan Bagna are great because people of all ages can prepare them - no excuses. They can be made several hours before you go on a picnic, or even the night before.

There are many variations on the fillings, so you can always experiment, but here are a couple of suggestions.

TUNA PAN BAGNA

You will need:

- 1 ciabatta loaf or French bread • 3 tbsp French dressing
  - fresh basil leaves • 3-4 large tomatoes
  - 2 hard-boiled eggs • ½ a 185g can of tuna
    - 8 pitted olives • 2 tbsp capers
      - 2 spring onions, chopped

 Cut the bread lengthways so that only one side is cut through while the other remains attached. (If using a baguette, cut in half first). Slice the tomatoes and eggs and cut the olives in half.

Sprinkle the insides of the bread with the dressing and cover with the fresh basil leaves. Layer the rest of the ingredients on top.

Close the loaf and wrap it tightly in plastic wrap. Then chill it in the fridge for at least two hours. Cut into portions before eating.

PAN BAGNA PROVENÇAL

You will need:

- 1 very large, round, country-style loaf or ciabatta
  - 100 g (4 oz) pesto • 120 ml (¼ pint) French dressing
    - 150 g (5 oz) salami • 4 large tomatoes, sliced
      - 10–20 pitted olives • 8 slices prosciutto ham

- 250 g (9 oz) fresh basil or rocket
- 250 g (9 oz) pepperdew chillies
  or pimentos in syrup, drained

If using a round loaf, slice off the top and keep it to serve as a lid. With a ciabatta, slice it lengthways so that only one side is cut through while the other remains attached.

Tear out the bread in the centre of the loaf, leaving a hollow 2 cm deep. Using a food processor, turn the bread into breadcrumbs and then mix half of them with the pesto. Mix the other half with the French dressing.

Add two-thirds of the pesto mix to the bottom half of the bread, then layer the salami, tomato, olives, French dressing mixture, prosciutto, basil or rocket, peppers and then the remainder of the pesto mix. Pack everything in and close the pan bagna.

Tightly wrap in plastic wrap and chill in the fridge. Finally unwrap and slice into portions.

A sharp knife is recommended to divide up the loaves but they can be broken with your hands – it just tends to be a bit messy.

Play The Letter Chain Game

This is a great way to liven up a long car journey. It is suitable for players of all ages. You can have as many people competing as you like.

Start by picking a category (one that matches the ability of all the players). Younger players might suit a category such as animals or food. Slightly older players might jump at the chance to name films, celebrities or countries.

The youngest player starts the game by naming an example of something that fits into the category, such as 'dog', if the subject is animals.

The second youngest player must then name an animal which begins with the last letter of the previous answer. For example: 'giraffe', because 'g' is the last letter of dog.

This continues until all players have given an answer in ascending order of age.

If a player gets stumped by his or her letter, they are out. The winner is the last person left in the game.

Play can then start again with a whole new subject and a whole new letter chain. Let your imagination run riot!

Top tip: When you've worked your way through all the obvious categories, experiment with a wide range of weird and wonderful subjects. How about imaginary creatures or storybook characters?

Stupendous Stained-Glass Window Biscuits

Here's how to create a stunning piece of edible art inside a biscuit. Unleash your imagination as you design your dazzling 'windows'.

You will need:

- 100 g (4 oz) caster sugar • 100 g (4 oz) butter or margarine • 225 g (9 oz) plain flour
- ½ tsp vanilla extract • juice and rind of ½ a lemon
- 1 egg yolk • boiled sweets in a selection of colours

Preheat the oven to gas mark 6/200°C/400°F.

Grease two baking sheets. Put the butter or margarine and the sugar into a large bowl, and mix together with a wooden spoon. When the mixture is soft and a light-yellow colour, add the flour, vanilla extract, grated lemon rind and the juice – then stir all the ingredients together.

Beat the egg yolk in a small bowl and then add it to the mixture. Combine to make a nice dough. Cover the dough in plastic wrap and put it in the fridge for 25 minutes.

Remove the dough from the fridge and on a very lightly floured surface, roll it out until it is about 1 cm thick.

Cut out your biscuits using a variety of cutter shapes.

Make a hole in each biscuit for a 'stained-glass window'. Experiment by cutting out various window shapes – try squares, hearts, circles, and even triangles. Use mini-cutter shapes if you have them. Place the biscuits on the baking sheets.

 Pop the biscuits in the oven and bake for six minutes. Then remove from the oven.

Now for the fun bit. Place a sweet in each of the cut-out shapes (being careful not to burn your hands on the hot biscuits or baking sheets).

 Put the biscuits back in the oven and cook for four more minutes or until the sweets start to melt. Remove the biscuits from the oven. Place on a wire rack and leave to cool.

Take a step back and admire your stained-glass treats.

Top tip: Stained-glass window biscuits make beautiful Christmas tree decorations. Make a hole in the top of each one before baking. When the biscuits have cooled, thread ribbon through the holes and tie them to your tree.

Make A Gorgeous Gift For Granny

This beautiful bath buff-puff is perfect for granny because not only does it look lovely, she'll find it very useful at bathtime for lathering up soap and shower gel.

Choose a pretty colour of netting and a matching ribbon to create a great gift.

You will need:

- 1 m soft tulle or netting • a needle with a large eye
- thread in a matching colour to the tulle
- ½ m pretty ribbon • pins

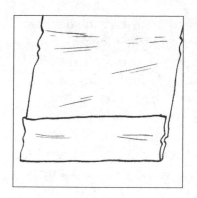

Spread the netting out flat. Fold the fabric over 12 cm up from the bottom edge. Fold over again and again until all the tulle has been folded into a tube 12 cm wide.

Secure the fabric with pins, and then sew along the centre of the tube from one end to the other using running stitch (see page 22).

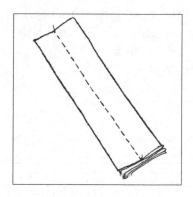

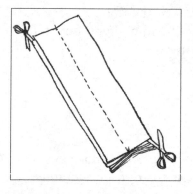

Once you have sewn along the length of the tulle, cut along both edges.

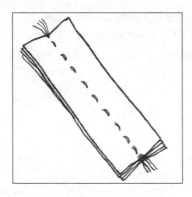

Using a loose running stitch, sew along the length of the tulle again, without securing your stitches at the end. The thread needs to be very strong for this so try quadrupling your thread (so that you are sewing with four strands instead of one).

Pull on the thread so that the tulle gathers together in a long ruffle. Secure at the end with a few stitches.

Finally stitch the two ends together to form a loop.

Attach the ribbon to the puff so it can be hung out to dry after use.

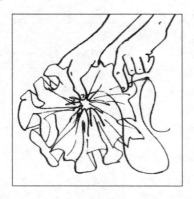

Now all you need to do is wrap it up with a bottle of bubbles and present it with a kiss to your lucky granny.

Twenty Questions

In this game one player thinks of an animal, plant or object and the other players must try and guess what it is by asking a maximum of twenty questions.

Each question can only be answered with a '*yes*' or a '*no*'. For example, you must not ask '*How many legs does it have?*' but you may ask '*Does it have four legs?*'

If the correct answer is guessed within the alloted number of questions the person who guesses wins the round and it is their turn to think of something.

Ornamental Eggshell Planter

When filled with cress, these planters are a great feature for a windowsill or a miniature garden (see pages 8 to 11). They also act as a miniature kitchen garden for Mum to pop on the windowsill, as the cress is delicious in sandwiches and salads.

You will need:

- 2 old egg cups (preferably matching)
- 2 eggs • cotton wool • cress seeds • acrylic paints

Boil the eggs for 4 minutes. Then, using a knife, remove the tops about one third of the way down. Scoop out the insides and serve with toast.

Carefully wash the eggshells to remove any lingering eggy bits and leave to dry.

Put the eggshells in the egg cups – open side up – and decorate them using acrylic paint (acrylic paint is waterproof when dry and will stop your design from running). Paint your eggs white or pale grey for a Grecian effect, or use a warm terracotta colour to give a more modern Mediterranean feel to your planters.

Leave the eggs to dry, and then remove them from the cups. Paint the egg cups to match your eggs.

When the egg cups are dry, pop in the shells – open side up. Put enough cotton wool into each planter so that it comes to about 1 cm from the top. Add just enough water to soak the cotton wool.

Sprinkle the wet cotton with cress seeds. Then place the finished planters in your miniature garden or on your windowsill.

Wait for the cress to sprout – this should take up to a week. Keep topping up your planters with water so that they don't dry out.

Create A Moving Easter Card

Pop-up cards are lots of fun and with this one the little chick opens and shuts its beak as if it is really tweeting! They are brilliant for Easter or, for a Christmas variation, you could draw a robin in a snowy scene. You could draw a ribbiting frog or even a friend who likes to talk a lot.

You will need:

- 2 pieces of thin card in different colours
- glue • scissors
- colouring pens, pencils or crayons

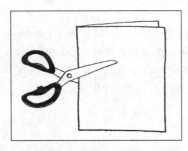

Fold one piece of card in half. Cut a line of about 5 cm across the middle of the crease.

Fold back each of the flaps to make two triangles, leaving a triangular hole at the crease. Sharpen the folds by running a fingernail along the folded edge of each triangle.

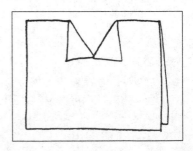

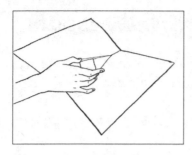

Unfold the triangles and open the card to about halfway.

Push one of the triangles through the hole and pinch to make it stand up. Repeat with the other triangle.

Close the card and press down on the folds to strengthen the creases. The 'beak' should now pop up when you open the card.

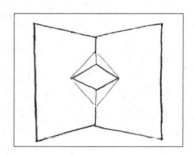

Fold the second piece of card and dab some glue around the inside edges. Stick the new piece of card to the back of your pop-up card, making sure none of the glue goes near the beak.

Now draw your bird around the beak and write your seasonal message.

Launch Orange Jelly Boats

Zing up dessert with a fantastic fleet of orange jelly boats. The perfect party pudding, just add ice cream.

You will need:

- 3 oranges • 1 pack fruit jelly
- 8 cocktail sticks • rice paper

Make up the jelly with hot water, following the instructions on the pack. To make a firmer jelly only use ¾ of the water suggested on the pack. Leave to cool until it is lukewarm. You can speed this up by adding a few ice cubes.

Meanwhile, cut the oranges in half using a sharp knife, and begin to loosen their insides by cutting round the inside edges. Be very careful not to pierce the skin of the orange or you will not be able to pour jelly into them.

Scoop out the rest of the insides of the orange halves using a spoon, trying to remove as much of the white membrane as possible.

Keep the empty orange halves steady by placing them in a bun tin and then fill each one to the top with the warm jelly mix. Put the bun tin containing your orange jellies in the fridge to set.

While waiting for your jelly boats to set, make the sails. Cut triangles about 6 cm high out of the rice paper and thread with cocktail sticks to act as masts.

When the jelly has set, cut the oranges again so that they are now in quarters. Arrange them on a plate – a blue one is best, or cover a plate with foil to look like glistening waves.

You are now ready to put up your sails and drift into the sunset.

Play Gods And Goddesses

This is a great game to get your mental cogs turning and to get you racking your brains for ancient celebrities and animals beginning with the letter Q.

Each player needs a sheet of paper and a pen. Divide the paper into a grid, with 11 boxes down the left-hand side and two columns wide enough to write four or five words in. At the top of the left-hand column write 'Category' and at the top of the right-hand column write 'Word'.

Now each player picks a category in turn and all players write them into the boxes in the left-hand column. Typical categories include TV programmes, authors, pop stars, trees, flowers, etc.

When ten categories are filled in, a letter is picked at random by someone sticking a pencil into the page of a newspaper, magazine or book with their eyes closed. Whichever letter the pencil is either touching or nearest to is the chosen letter for the round.

Timing with a watch or timer, one player says 'Go'. Players now have two minutes to fill in as many of the categories as they can with answers beginning with the chosen letter.

Where the answer is a person's name, the surname should begin with the correct letter.

Opposite is an example of what the sheet may look like.

The chosen letter is 'S'.

CATEGORY	WORD
Trees	Sycamore
Popstars/groups	Britney Spears
Film stars	Sylvester Stallone
Authors	William Shakespeare
Books	Swallows and Amazons
Gods and Goddesses	Saturn
Countries	Spain
Animals	Sheep
TV programmes	Sesame Street
Flowers	Snowdrop

If anyone fills their sheet in before the 2 minutes are up, they can shout 'Stop' and the round ends. Otherwise all players must stop writing after 2 minutes.

Scores are determined by the number of people who have the same answer as you for each category. The top score is ten but one point is knocked off for each person who duplicates your answer. E.g. if three people have the answer 'Snowdrop', each player only scores seven for that answer.

A new letter is then chosen for the next round.

Make Your Own Lemonade

On a baking hot summer's day there's nothing more refreshing than a large jug of homemade lemonade.

You will need:

- 7 lemons (to make a slightly sweeter drink, replace one of the lemons with a large orange)
- 350 g caster sugar • 1½ litres water
- runny honey to taste

Grate the zest of two of the lemons into a large saucepan. Pour over 1½ litres of water and add the sugar.

 Heat the lemon, water and sugar mixture until all of the sugar has dissolved and leave to cool.

Squeeze the juice of all the lemons into a large jug. Pour the cooled water over the lemon juice and stir.

Each time you make lemonade the flavour will be slightly different so always taste the mixture before serving. Stir in a teaspoon of honey if necessary. Add some ice cubes to the jug and serve.

Top tip: To make pink lemonade, add a cup of cranberry juice. This gives your drink a nice tang and makes it a lovely colour.

Make A Denim Kit Bag

Denim bags are great, lightweight, washable holdalls and seriously trendy too. Instead of paying a fortune for one in a shop, find an old pair of jeans and recycle them into this must-have accessory. Make sure nobody wants the jeans first though – you don't want to take the scissors to Dad's new designer denims without asking.

You will need:

- an old pair of jeans • scissors • chalk or pen
- ruler • a brightly coloured cotton or silk scarf
- optional embellishments

Zip up the jeans and turn them inside out. Lay them out flat in front of you, bottom side up, and measure 2½ cm down the leg from the crotch.

With chalk, draw a line across the leg at this mark and repeat for the other leg. Cut the legs off at the line you have drawn.

Sew each leg closed 2½ cm from the cut edge. Trim the seam to 1 cm, then turn the bag so it is right side out.

To make a handle, thread a brightly coloured scarf through the belt loops and tie the ends together. Alternatively, cut the two inside seams from the leftover legs of the jeans and sew onto both sides of the bag to make long handles.

Now add any embellishments you like, such as fabric football badges, swimming or gymnastic awards as well as buttons or ribbons. Stitch them into place for a truly original design.

Make Chocolate Leaves

Chocolate leaves make impressive and delicious decorations for cakes or desserts.

You will need:

- 115 g plain chocolate
- non-toxic leaves such as rose, lemon or bay leaves
- a pastry brush
- greaseproof paper

Carefully wash the leaves and pat them dry using a clean tea towel.

Cover your work surface with a sheet of newspaper to protect it from any stray dribbles of chocolate, and lay some greaseproof paper on a tray ready for your leaves.

Break the chocolate into chunks in a glass bowl.

Melt the chocolate either on low power in the microwave, or over a pan of boiling water, stirring until it is runny.

When the chocolate has melted, remove it from the heat. Use a table knife or pastry brush to spread a thick and even layer of chocolate on the underside (the bumpy side) of each leaf. Take care not to go over the edges or your leaves will be difficult to peel off later.

Place the leaves, chocolate side up, on the tray lined with greaseproof paper or over a rolling pin to give them a nice curl. Put them in the fridge for about an hour.

Take the leaves out of the fridge. Holding the stalk, gently peel the leaf away from the chocolate. Don't worry if some of your leaves break at this stage. With patience and practice you will have forests of them!

Refrigerate the chocolate leaves in an airtight container until you can resist them no longer.

Brilliant Butterfly Magnets

Use coffee filters to make the multicoloured wings of a butterfly. The resulting butterflies can be made into a fridge magnet or a brooch, or clipped onto curtains or fabric around the house.

You will need:

• a round coffee filter • food colouring in various colours • a pipette or small paintbrush • cake tin • clean yogurt pots or any small containers • pipe cleaners • a wooden clothes peg • black or brown paint • small magnet or magnetic strip, or safety pin (for brooch) • strong glue

In the yogurt pots or small containers, mix six drops of food colouring with a few drops of water (make sure you don't dilute it too much).

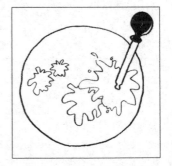

Put a coffee filter in the bottom of a cake tin. Using the pipette or paintbrush, drip the coloured water onto the filter, allowing it to spread.

Do the same with another colour, then another and so on, making different coloured blobs all over the paper. Leave to dry.

Paint the clothes peg black or brown and leave to dry.

Fold a pipe cleaner into a V-shape and glue to the flat end of the clothes peg (the bit you pinch). This forms the antennae of the butterfly.

Scrunch the filter in the middle, to form wings and then clip the clothes peg onto the middle. Tease the paper into wing shapes.

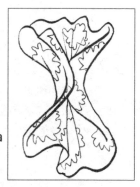

Glue magnetic tape or a magnet to the back of your butterfly and stick it on the fridge. Alternatively, attach a safety pin using sticky tape to make a brooch.

If you can't find any safety pins (because no one can find a safety pin when they need one), clip the clothes peg to your curtains.

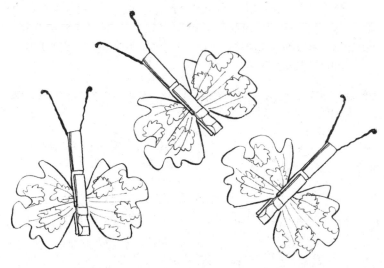

Pasta And Rice Pictures

Raid the food cupboard and create pictures with a difference. Pasta and rice with an added dash of colour make great materials for getting arty, but it can get messy. Put a mat or some old newspaper down before you start.

You will need:

- rice • pasta of various shapes e.g. farfalle (bows), macaroni, fusilli (twists) and penne (tubes)
- food colouring • paper • craft or PVA glue
- a pen or pencil

Place some of the pasta in a resealable plastic bag with a few drops of food colouring. Seal the bag, shake and then turn out the pasta onto newspaper to dry. Don't shake so hard that you shatter the pasta – just enough to spread the colour around.

Repeat with as many different colours and pasta shapes as you wish.

To colour the rice, divide it into various bowls (margarine tubs or old yogurt pots will do just as well) and then add a drop or two of food colouring into each. Stir in thoroughly. Add more food colouring if you want to increase the strength of the colour. Spread the rice out on newspaper to dry.

Put the coloured pasta and rice into separate bowls in the middle of your kitchen table.

Draw a picture and then glue on the pasta shapes and rice. If you prefer you could miss out the drawing stage and just go with the flow in the tradition of all great abstract artists.

Leave the paper flat until the glue is dry to prevent your picture falling off the page.

Warning! Even when they are dry these works of art tend to shed the odd pasta bow and sprinkle rice on the carpet. But you have to suffer for your art.

Make A Haunted House

Get crafting at Halloween and create your very own
haunted house – perfect for spooking visitors and great
just for a little October fun.

You will need:

• an empty shoe box • white tissue paper
• cotton thread • scissors • a glue stick • sticky tape
• black poster paint • a sizeable lump of modelling clay
• a sharp pencil • a ruler

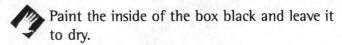

Cut away one end of the shoe box completely, saving the
piece of card for later on.

Position the opposite end of the box over the piece
of modelling clay and use the point of a pencil to
make a hole in the middle of the cardboard.

Paint the inside of the box black and leave it
to dry.

Cut out an oblong of tissue paper, slightly larger than the
end of the box and tape it over the open end.

Sketch the shape of a bat, a ghost and a cat on the spare
piece of card from the end of the shoe box. Cut them out
and paint them black. Put them to one side to dry.

When dry, use the point of the pencil to make a hole in the top of each of your scary shapes, pushing through the card into the modelling clay underneath. In the same way, make three holes on each of the long sides of the shoe box in the positions shown.

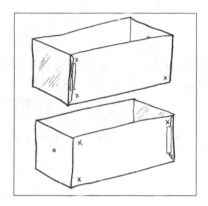

Measure and cut two pieces of cotton that are twice the width of the box and one piece that is twice the length of the box. Thread the longest piece of cotton through the top of the hat and secure with a knot in the centre. Then repeat with the cat and ghost pieces.

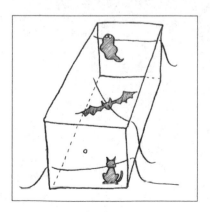

Thread the cat between the two lowest holes at the front of the shoe box and then string the ghost between the two highest holes at the back. Lastly, thread the bat diagonally across the box between the remaining holes.

Tie a loop at each end of the pieces of cotton and use them to pull the spooky characters back and forth inside the box. Replace the lid.

Place your haunted house near a good source of light – a window is fine during the day, a lamp in the evening. Now choose a victim and spook them out, by getting them to look through the spy hole while you pull the characters back and forth. You could even make up scary stories to tell while you do it.

Make A Super Scrunchie

Use your brand new sewing skills learned on pages 22 to 24 to make a fabulous hair accessory. Making your own accessories means you can match them exactly to your outfit. Scrunchies are great to make as gifts or to sell at the school fête.

You will need:

• fabric measuring 42 cm x 13 cm • elastic – width ½ cm, length 26 cm • 2 safety pins • needle and thread

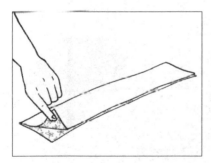

Fold the fabric over along the long side, so that only the underside shows.

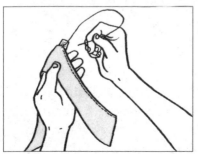

Using backstitch (see page 23) sew along the open edge about 2 cm in. Turn the fabric tube right side out.

Pin one of the safety pins to the end of the elastic and attach it to one end of the tube.

Pin the other pin to the opposite end of the elastic and thread the elastic through the tube.

Undo the safety pins, without letting go of the two ends of the elastic and then tie a secure knot, leaving 5 cm of elastic at the ends. Tuck the ends inside the material. Fold over the cut edges of the scrunchie fabric. Sew the two ends of the fabric tube together.

Host A Clothes-Swap Party

Everyone has clothes in their wardrobe they have outgrown or never wear. However, one person's fashion faux-pas is another's fashion find of the century. Why not clear out and refresh your wardrobe by hosting a clothes-swap party? Hand-me-downs are nowhere near as horrible if they come from that cool, older kid from down the road.

You will need:

• invitations • guests
• party food and drink • paper (in three different colours)

Pick a date and compose invitations a few weeks beforehand. Here is an example, but you can word it however you wish:

Dear ....

We have decided it is time for an image update and were hoping you could help. Please join us for an evening of fashion exchange, fun and food on (insert date).

Please bring at least five items of clothing that you are prepared to part with. All items must be clean and in good condition.

The clothes swap will commence at 7pm.

RSVP: (Insert your names/phone number).

When the day of the party arrives work together to prepare drinks and nibbles. You also need to prepare the room for the swap. Create three areas for clothes. For example, you can divide them into tops, bottoms and accessories. If there are few accessories, substitute those for shoes, or whichever three categories you think will give the most equal distribution. If you want, you could also divide adults' and children's clothing. Allocate a ticket colour to each area.

When your guests arrive make sure you put their coats in another room so they don't end up being part of the swap. Get your guests to put their swap clothes into the appropriate areas. Write a ticket out for each item and person. For example, if tops are in the yellow area, and your guest adds a top to the pile, write your guest's name on a yellow ticket.

Put all the tickets into a large bowl and shake them up. You then take it in turns to pick tickets out of the bowl. The person whose name is on the ticket can then choose an item from the appropriate coloured pile. For example, if your yellow ticket is picked, you can choose a top from the pile in the yellow area.

Top tip: To add a bit more excitement to the proceedings, add the following rule. If an item is chosen, and another person wants it, they can raise a hand and say '*I object*'. A game of scissors, paper, stone or the toss of a coin can then be used to determine who gets the item.

Make sure your friends know all the rules before you begin swapping, and explain that some people may end up with a few things they don't want as this is the nature of the swap. These can be collected at the end of the party, bagged up and taken to a local charity shop.

Plan The Perfect Picnic

What could be more fun on a bright sunny day, than a picnic? The great thing about picnics is that you can have one almost anywhere – in the park, in the woods, on a village green or even in your garden. Food always tastes better outdoors. The only rule should be that everyone has to help prepare the food.

Check the weather forecast the day before you plan on having a picnic. If the forecast is too cold or rainy, why not have a carpet picnic indoors instead?

Don't despair if there isn't a traditional picnic basket to hand, but do make sure you have other suitable storage for your food and drink. Cool bags are excellent for keeping food and drinks chilled.

Take something to sit on. Unless you're heading to a picnic spot with chairs and tables provided, you'll need a blanket or groundsheet to put your food on and to sit down on. Take a few cushions for extra comfort.

When picking a picnic spot always make sure you are allowed to picnic there.

Take a plastic bag with you to put any rubbish in and take it with you when you leave. Always clear up behind you after you have finished and leave the picnic spot just as you found it.

Top tips: Make your picnic even more fun by giving it a theme. Invite lots of friends and have a competition to see who brings the most popular dish.

Outdoor games are a great way to liven up a picnic.
Try Giddy Running (see pages 126 to 127) or a game of
Wildlife Bingo (see pages 108 to 109).

Here is a recipe for picnic pastries that are easy to eat
alfresco.

MOUTH-WATERING PICNIC PASTRIES

These cheese parcels are great for a picnic as they taste
really delicious when eaten cold. They are also lovely when
still warm from the oven.

You will need:

For the pastry:
- 225 g (8 oz) plain flour • ½ tsp salt
- 100 g (4 oz) butter or margarine
- 2-3 tbsp cold water • 1 beaten egg

For the filling:
- 200 g (7 oz) boiled new potatoes, cut into cubes
- 200 g (7 oz) cheddar cheese, cut into cubes
- 1 leek, boiled and sliced

First mix the flour and salt in a bowl. Then cut the margarine or butter into small pieces and rub it into the flour until the mixture resembles breadcrumbs. Add the water, a little bit at a time, and knead until the mixture forms a soft pastry dough.

Cover the bowl with plastic wrap and place in the fridge for an hour.

Meanwhile, make the cheesy filling by mixing the cheese, potatoes and leeks in bowl.

After an hour, roll out the pastry on a clean, floured surface until it is 3 mm thick. Cut out pastry circles, using a side plate (about 15 cm in diameter) as a template. Alternatively, divide the pastry into four parts and roll each piece into a circle of the same diameter.

Put a spoonful of filling in the middle of each circle. Fold the edges of the circle together over the top of the filling, crimping them together with your fingers to form an enclosed pasty shape.

 Place your pastries on a baking sheet and brush them with the egg. Bake them in the oven at gas mark 6/200°C/400°F for 20 minutes, or until golden brown.

Let the pastries cool before placing them in an airtight container all ready for your picnic. Alternatively, enjoy them while they are still toasty-warm as you picnic on your carpet!

Warning: The filling inside these pastries stays hot for longer than you think, so make sure you test the centre with a knife before taking a bite.

Play Wildlife Bingo

Turn an everyday walk in the park or countryside into a nail-biting adventure by playing Wildlife Bingo.

Before leaving the house find a sheet of paper for each walker and divide it into a grid of 9, 12 or 16 squares.

In each square of the grid draw or write the name of an animal or plant that you might spot on the walk. For example, if you are walking in woods you could include types of birds, flowers, mammals and trees that you are likely to see.

Make each sheet different so that not all the animals and plants are the same. If players are of different ages, you should think about putting the easier things to find on the younger ones' sheets, and for older or more experienced players you should be more specific as to the wildlife they have to spot, e.g. a certain species of wild flower or fungus.

Give each player a pen and a grid, and as you walk along mark off each item as you see it.

Make sure everyone knows when the game has begun, so that they don't start marking their card early. There must be a witness to each sighting whenever possible. Continue on the walk very quietly and carefully, making sure you don't miss or scare off any possible sightings.

The first player to cross off everything on their grid wins the game and says 'Bingo!' Be careful not to shout though, as you don't want to scare any of the animals off for the next game.

Make sure your bingo grids are seasonal and in keeping with your environment – there is no point in spending the day hunting for an autumn leaf in the spring or looking for a grizzly bear at the beach.

Cheer Up Your China

Spruce up old plates or mugs with your own stylish designs. If you don't have any spare plates or mugs about the house, have a look through your local charity shop. There are sure to be some bits of crockery crying out for a makeover.

You will need:

- paper • colouring pencils or felt-tips
- a plain plate, mug or bowl • brushes • newspapers
- ceramic paints (found online or in craft shops)

Top tip: If you are planning to use your redecorated item for food or drink, check that the ceramic paint you use is safe for contact with food.

Have a look in some art or antiques books to get inspiration. You could make a striking, colourful design like Picasso or a more refined 'blue willow' pattern. Alternatively, you could make personalized mugs for your friends and family.

Test out a few designs on paper, using colouring pencils or felt-tips first. This way you can decide the effect you want without messing up your crockery.

Wash and dry your plate thoroughly, to remove any greasy fingerprints or residue that could stop the paint from sticking to the surface.

Lay out your paints, brushes and the item to be painted on a surface protected with newspaper or a mat. Sketch out your design onto the plate using a pencil and then off you go.

When you have finished painting, leave your masterpiece to dry overnight to make sure your design has completely set.

Before you can use your plate, most ceramic paints need to be baked in the oven. For this, follow the manufacturer's instructions given on the side of the paint pots. Make sure you let your work of art cool after baking and wash again before use.

Top tip: Why stop at plates? You could do flower pots, egg cups, ceramic toast-racks or vases. Many ceramic paints can also be used on glass, so why not personalize your own drinking glass or make one for a friend?

Salt-Dough Decorations

Have a little festive fun and brighten up your Christmas tree with some unique home-made ornaments. Salt-dough decorations can also be made into fridge magnets to bring Christmas to the kitchen. To up the Christmas factor even more, pop on a seasonal CD while you work. Don't eat the dough though – it tastes horrible.

You will need:

- 100 g (3½ oz) salt • 140 g (5 oz) flour • 115 ml water
- star and Christmas tree pastry cutters • a cocktail stick
  - acrylic paints in red, green, yellow and other
    colours of your choice
  - glitter glue • ribbon or string

Mix together the salt, flour and water in a large bowl until you have made a sticky dough and there are no dry floury bits.

Sprinkle some flour on your work surface and knead the dough by squashing it with your knuckles, until it is smooth. If the dough is sticky, sprinkle it with a little more flour. Make sure you don't add too much, or the dough will get too dry and crack.

Dust a rolling pin with flour and roll out the dough until it is a ½ cm thick. Use the pastry cutters to cut out as many shapes as you can. If you haven't got pastry cutters draw a cardboard template and use a knife to cut round the shape.

With a cocktail stick, make a hole for the ribbon near the top of each shape (not too close to the edge).

Place the shapes on to a baking sheet and bake for two hours in a very low oven (Gas mark ½/130°C/250°F).

Place the baked decorations on a wire rack to cool.

Paint the cooled decorations in seasonal colours. Leave them to dry.

When the paint is dry, cover with glitter glue to make them sparkle.

Finally, thread the ribbon (or string) through the hole and hang on your tree.

If you want to make a fridge magnet, don't make a hole in the ornament. When the decoration is finished, glue a small magnet (as found in most craft shops) on to the back.

Top tip: Why wait until Christmas? Salt-dough figures can be made any time. Make heart-shapes to hang on door handles or the initials of family members to stick on their bedroom doors.

Seriously Super Smoothies

A smoothie will provide goodness for your insides as well as tasting super. Shop-bought smoothies are usually expensive, but this quick, simple drink is far cheaper made with fresh natural ingredients packed with vitamins and totally yummy.

You will need:

- 1 small tub of fruit yogurt • 1 glass of milk
- 1 ripe banana • a handful of soft fruit (strawberries, raspberries and blackberries work particularly well)

Slice the banana and put into a blender or liquidiser. Add the yogurt and fruit and blend for a minute. Add the milk and blend for a few seconds more. Pour and enjoy!

Make A Prickly Hedgehog

This pin-covered pet is a practical pal in anyone's sewing box. Either keep him all to yourself, or give him to a friend or relative. He may look cute but don't give him a cuddle or you could get pricked.

You will need:

- black and brown felt
- 2 buttons or teddy bear eyes from a craft shop
- scissors • chalk • needle and black thread
- tracing paper and pencil
- old tights or more fabric scraps for stuffing

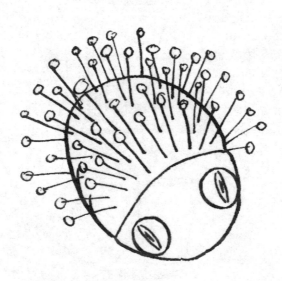

First you need to make the pattern for your prickly friend. Place the tracing paper over the pattern below and draw around it using a pencil. Trace around each shape separately so that you end up with three shapes on your paper. Cut these out carefully using scissors.

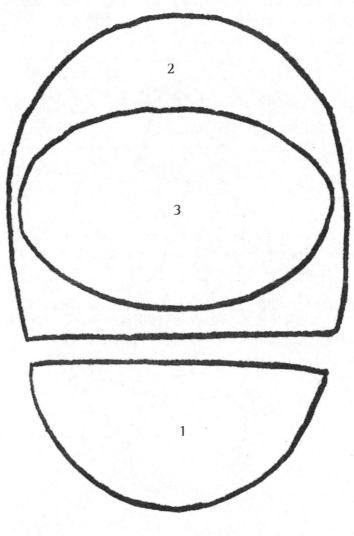

Place shape 1 onto a piece of black felt and draw around it with chalk. Repeat this on the brown felt with shapes 2 and 3 and then cut out your shapes.

Using running stitch (see page 22), sew felt shape 1 to felt shape 2 along the straight edge as shown. Secure your stitches at the beginning and end of sewing with a few stitches on top of each other.

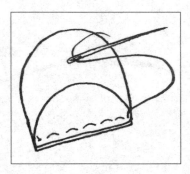

Sew the black and brown top piece to felt shape 3 with the seam facing inwards so that the seam will be inside your pincushion.

Gather the edges of the top piece as you sew to make them fit together. Stop before you have sewn all the way around, leaving hole to insert the stuffing.

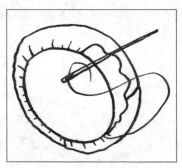

Fill your cushion with stuffing until it is firm and then sew up the hole.

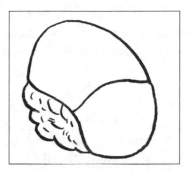

Sew on the buttons for your hedgehog's eyes.

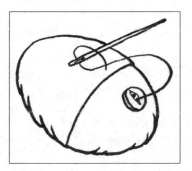

All that's missing now are his prickles, so fill the hedgehog with all of your pins.

Make The Perfect Omelette

Omelettes are the original fast food and can provide a filling, nutritious meal in minutes. Simple as they seem, it's easy to make them too stodgy or too thin.

You will need:

- 3 eggs
- a pinch of mixed herbs
- a knob of butter
- a 20 cm frying pan (15 cm for a two-egg omelette)
- salt and pepper

Break the eggs into a bowl, add the salt, pepper and herbs and then beat the egg mixture lightly with a fork.

Place the pan over a medium heat. Add the butter and then tilt the pan over the heat so that the melting butter coats the bottom.

Turn up the heat and pour in the beaten eggs.

Allow the mixture to set a little and then use a spatula to push it away from the sides. Tip the pan so that any uncooked egg on top runs to the edges. When the top is almost cooked, take the spatula and fold the omelette in half. Tip it on to a warm plate and serve immediately.

Top tip: Once you have mastered the perfect omelette, experiment with different fillings. Any of the following ingredients can be added to the egg mixture:

• chopped ham • chopped cooked bacon • grated cheese – approximately 25 g (1 oz) per egg • chopped tomatoes • potatoes, pre-cooked and chopped

Top tip: The key to a light, fluffy omelette is making sure the butter is hot before you add the eggs and always using the right-sized pan.

Grow An Avocado Plant

Avocados make beautiful indoor plants and will grow from the stone of the fruit you eat.

You will need:

- a few ripe avocados • a knife
- some jars or wide-necked bottle
- water • cocktail sticks • a 15 cm plant pot
- potting compost • sand

Top tip: Not all avocado stones will grow into successful plants so it pays to have a few spares.

Cut open an avocado by piercing the skin and then running the knife around the stone, being careful not to damage it. Open gently and remove the stone. Scoop out the flesh and enjoy later – or make Avocado Ghouls (see page 56 and 57).

Wash the stone and insert three cocktails sticks into its side. The cocktail sticks should be evenly spaced and about halfway down from the widest end.

Using the cocktail sticks as a rest, suspend the stone pointed side up, in a jar filled with water. Place the jar on a warm windowsill. Keep the jar filled to the brim with water at all times, so that half of the stone is underwater.

In two or three weeks, the stone will crack. In another four weeks a root will grow from the submerged end. Shortly afterwards a stem will begin to grow.

When the root is at least 5 cm long and the stem is at least 10 cm tall, plant the stone in a pot measuring 15 cm or more in diameter. Good potting soil should be used – mix three parts of soil with one part of sand. The pot should be kept wet for the first week. After that the soil should be watered once a week and kept moist.

Avocado plants can grow into small bushes or taller trees. Which one is up to you. If you want a bush, pinch off the tip of the plant and the tips of new branches and more branches will grow. If you would prefer a small tree, just let it grow upwards.

Don't wait around for your plant to bear fruit though, as it could take years or it may never happen at all.

Knot A Scoubidou Key Ring

Get knotting and make a really cool key ring – all it takes is a little practice.

You'll need:

- 2 different-coloured scoubie strands
- a split ring that takes keys
- a medium-sized bead (match it with your scoubie colours, if you can)

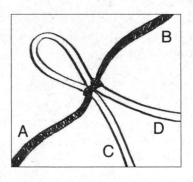

Step 1. Make a small loop in the middle of one strand and then tie the different coloured strand around the loop in a knot. This will be the loop you attach the split ring to.

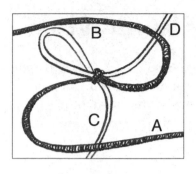

Step 2. You now have four scoubie strands, A and B in one colour, C and D in a second colour. Arrange the colours so that they are opposite each other in a cross.

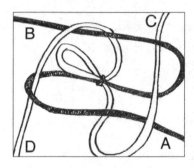

Step 3. Make a loop in strand A and a loop in strand B as shown. Now thread strand C through loop A and strand D through loop B and pull tight. The knot should now look like a chequered square.

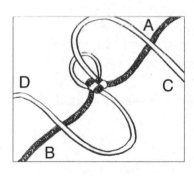

Step 4. Repeat step three, but this time make loops with strand C and strand D and then thread A and B through the loops you have made and tighten.

Continue your scoubie, alternating the knots made in steps 3 and 4 until it is as long as you want. Leave a 6 cm length at the end of each strand. To add a bead, thread your bead over all four strands before making a final knot.

Play Giddy Running

The only thing more fun than getting as dizzy as you can and then trying to walk in a straight line is watching someone else do it. A good game for the garden, make sure you have lots of soft cushions so that you don't land with too much of a bump.

You will need:

- a large, flat grassy space in a garden or park
- lots of pillows and soft things to land on
- a broom handle or stick

Lay the cushions out in two straight lines about a metre apart. This will mark the course.

Stand at the beginning of the course and hold the broom handle or stick to your chest vertically, so that the end of it comes about 30 cm above your head. Look up at the end of the broom and spin round as fast as you can five times. The other players should count out loud as you spin.

Stop when you are facing the beginning of the course and drop the broom carefully to the side. Now try to walk (or run) as fast as you can in a straight line to the end of the course. This is not as easy as you think, as you will now be very dizzy and will probably stumble as soon as you make a start.

The aim of giddy running is to get as far along the course as possible without touching the pillows at the side, and if you reach the end, to run back.

Classic Card Games

Playing cards is a great rainy-day activity that should never be forgotten or underestimated.

TWO-HAND WHIST

This simple form of whist can be played with two or more players.

The dealer deals seven cards to each player and then cuts the pack to determine which suit is 'trumps'. The object of the game is to win as many 'tricks' as possible. A trick is where each player has had one turn. There are seven tricks available in each hand.

The other player (or the player to the left of the dealer if there are more than two of you) then lays a card in the

middle of the table. Players must lay a card of the same suit if possible and the highest card wins the trick.

However, if a player can't follow suit they can lay any suit they like. If they lay a 'trump' i.e. any card from the trump suit, that card will beat all non-trump cards. A trump card can be beaten only by another, higher trump card.

For example, if spades are trumps, a king of diamonds can be beaten by a two of spades. The two of spades can, in turn, be beaten by the three of spades or any higher spade.

The winner of the trick takes the cards and lays them face down on the table, and then leads the next trick.

Aces are always high. The winner of each round is the player who wins the most tricks.

KNOCKOUT WHIST

This game is exactly the same as Two-Hand Whist, except that you need more than two players, as any player who fails to win a trick is knocked out.

As a variation you can reduce the number of cards dealt by one each hand, starting at seven and reducing, eventually, to one.

The winner is the last surviving player when the others are knocked out.

UP AND DOWN THE RIVER

This game is based on whist but, instead of winning as many tricks as possible, you must predict the number of tricks you will win by looking at your hand.

For the first hand, the dealer deals one card each and then cuts to determine which suit is trumps. Each player must predict the number of tricks they can win (one or zero in this case) with the dealer bidding last. The total number of tricks predicted by each player MUST add up to either more or less than the possible amount for the hand. For example, if only one trick has already been bid for in round one, the dealer cannot bid zero, but must bid one no matter what their cards. This forces someone to lose the round.

If a player's prediction is right, he or she scores ten points plus the number of tricks bid. If their bid is over or under, the player scores only the amount of tricks won.

The number of cards dealt increases by one card each time, up to a total of seven.

After the round with seven cards is finished, there are several novelty rounds. Still playing with seven cards, try the following variations:

Half-blind. Players bid on their hand before they know the trump suit.

Blind. Players must bid before seeing their hand or cutting for trumps.

Misère. Three penalty points are deducted from a player's score for each trick they win, so you need to get as few as you can. Players who win no tricks gain ten points.

When these three rounds are finished, the game continues back 'down the river' from seven cards to one.

The winner is the player with the highest score.

Make Fortune Cookies

Fortune cookies are delicious cookies with a surprise inside. They are great fun at parties and can be even more fun if you write your own fortunes to put in them.

You will need:

- 2 egg whites • ½ tsp vanilla extract
- 1 pinch salt • 35 g (1¼ oz) flour
- 50 g (1¾ oz) white sugar
- a sheet of plain paper • a pen/pencil

THE FORTUNES

Before you start to cook, cut the paper into strips of around 7½ cm by 1 cm so they are slim enough to fit inside the cookies.

Write your fortunes. Make them as general as possible as you don't know who will pick which cookie. Never put bad fortunes in as they might be taken seriously.

Traditional messages include, 'You will live long and prosper', or 'Seven will be your lucky number this weekend'.

THE COOKIES

Put the egg whites in a large bowl with the vanilla extract. Whisk until fluffy but not stiff. Add the flour, salt and sugar and mix together.

Place teaspoonfuls of the batter 10 cm apart on a baking sheet and tilt so that they make circles of about 7½ cm in diameter.

Bake for 5 minutes at gas mark 6/200°C/400°F or until the cookies are golden at the edges. In the meantime, prepare the next sheet and put these in the oven when the first batch is ready.

Take the cookies out of the oven and quickly remove them with a wide spatula, placing upside down on a wooden board. Put the fortune onto the cookie, close to the middle, and fold the cookie in half.

Holding the folded cookie in both hands, between your thumb and index fingers, fold in half again so that it is in quarters. If your cookie is a little stiff pull the ends down over the rim of a glass or the handle of a wooden spoon, until the ends meet. The opened side of the fortune cookie should be facing upwards, towards you.

Always use cold baking sheets, as warm ones will make them cook too quickly.

You must work fast with the cookies in the final stages as the cookies set very quickly. For best results do three or four cookies at a time.

Top tip: If you can find a pair of cotton gloves to help you touch the cookies when they are hot, it will help.

Make Your Own Craft Kit

There's no need to buy an expensive kit from a craft shop – make your own. Start by designing the box you want to keep your kit in. Cover a shoe box in wrapping paper or decoupage (see pages 146 to 148). Better still, cover with fabric as described below for a stunning transformation.

FABRIC COVERED BOX

You will need:

- 1 shoe box with lid • 1 m of fabric
- spray adhesive or strong craft glue • scissors
- sheet of upholstery foam or wadding for lid (optional)

Measure around all four sides of the box, then add 2½ cm to the total length. Measure the depth and, again, add 2½ cm.

Draw a long rectangle using these measurements on a sheet of paper and cut it out. Then pin your template to the fabric and cut round it.

Place the bottom of the box on to the fabric and draw around it. Cut out this rectangle and put to one side (you will use this to cover the bottom of the box once the sides have been covered).

Spray or paint a thin layer of glue onto one of the long sides of the box and smooth on the longer rectangle of fabric. Make sure you leave a little fabric at the top and bottom to turn over at the end to make neat edges.

Now move around the box, applying glue to each side and carefully smoothing on the fabric. Try not to leave any creases or air bubbles under the material.

When you reach the end, fold the remainder of the material under itself and glue down, so that the fabric joins neatly at the corner.

At the top corners, cut narrow triangles in the overlapping fabric and stick down to the inside of the box.

Turn the box over, spray or spread glue over the bottom of the box and smooth on the smaller rectangle of fabric.

Place the lid of your box on to your fabric and draw around this. Measure the depth of the lid and add this to the edge of each of the lid's sides plus an extra 2½ cm to tuck under. If you would like a padded lid, glue the foam or wadding to the lid of the box first.

Cut the fabric rectangle for the lid and then apply glue to the top of the lid or padding and stick on your fabric.

Glue the fabric to the long sides and then fold down at the corners and glue on to the short sides. Finish by cutting small triangles in the corners of overlapping material and glueing the fabric down inside.

ITEMS FOR YOUR KIT

Now you have a beautiful box to keep your collage and design materials in, so here are a few suggestions for the contents:

- fabric scraps • ribbons • paper • pens
- buttons • beads • straws • string
- ice-lolly sticks • glitter • glitter glue
- wrapping paper • silver foil • wallpaper
- magazine cuttings • gift bows

Keep lidded pots, such as those that poster paints come in, for storing beads, buttons and other items. If anyone you know has a non-digital camera, ask them for the empty film cases, which are really useful, and keep the little tubes that you buy glitter and craft materials in for re-use.

Disguise The Spy

Make your own undercover agent and dress him for top secret missions. This message will self distruct in 60 seconds ...

You will need:

- a photocopier or tracing paper and a pencil
- card • glue • scissors • sticky-backed plastic
- felt-tip pens

Photocopy pages 138 and 139, enlarging them if you wish. If you do not have access to a photocopier, trace around the items using tracing paper and a pencil.

Glue the spy to a piece of card and colour him in and cover with sticky-backed plastic. Cut him out carefully and fold along the dotted line to make him able to stand.

To make his basic spy clothes, colour and cut out his hat, coat and trousers. Fit them to his body using the tabs.

Your spy is now ready to begin his investigations, however, he will need more clothes in order to remain undercover. Decide on his mission: he could need to locate an enemy agent at a disco or even head off into space.

Draw your designs on paper and colour in before cutting out. Include short tabs on each garment which can fold over the spy's outline.

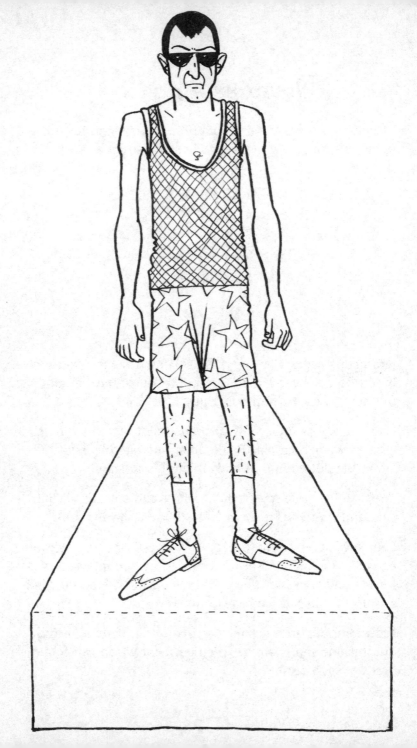

Banana Loaf

A banana loaf is a huge family favourite and perfect for any picnic.

You will need:

- 450 g (1 lb soft bananas (around 3 large ones)
- 225 g (8 oz) self-raising flour
- 100 g (4 oz) butter
- 150 g (5 oz) caster sugar
- ½ tsp salt • 2 eggs
- 225 g (8 oz) mixed dried fruit
- a 900 g (2 lb) loaf tin, lightly greased

Preheat the oven to gas mark 4/180°C/350°F.

 While the oven is warming up, peel the bananas and mash them with a fork in a large bowl.

Add the rest of the ingredients, except for the dried fruit. Mix until thoroughly blended, then add the dried fruit and mix again.

Pour the mixture into your loaf tin and bake in the oven for 1½ hours.

You can tell if the loaf is properly cooked by pushing a metal skewer or knife into the middle of it. If it comes out clean, your banana loaf is done.

Cool on a wire rack.

Make Your Very Own Teddy Mascot

Why buy a cuddly toy from a shop, when you can create a cute companion unlike any other? Here's how to make a lovable friend that will bring you luck.

You will need:

- a photocopier or tracing paper and a pencil
- 35 cm x 35 cm fur fabric and matching thread
- two pieces of cardboard (A4)
- eyes and nose (found in craft shops), or black buttons
- black embroidery thread
- a needle • some pins • stuffing or old tights
- scissors • a felt-tip pen • glue

TED'S TEMPLATES

Start by photocopying the front and back pattern from pages 144 and 145. If you do not have access to a photocopier, trace the patterns. Glue the patterns on to cardboard and leave to dry. When the glue is dry, cut around the outline of the pattern to make your ted templates.

Place the front template on the back of the furry fabric and draw around it with the felt tip. When you have drawn around one side, turn the template over and draw around it the other way. This wil give your bear a right and a left side. Repeat this with the template for the back of the bear.

Cut out your pieces. You should end up with four pieces – two front and two back.

IT'S SEW TIME

With the furry sides of the fabric facing each other, pin the front pieces of the bear together. Sew the two pieces together down the middle from point A to point B, using backstitch (see page 23), leaving a seam of ½ cm around the edge. Do the same with the back section, sewing this time from point C to D, leaving an opening in the back seam, as shown on the pattern.

If using a nose and eyes from a craft shop, affix them to the front of the bear now, following the instructions on the pack.

Pin the back section to the front – furry sides together – and sew around the outsides. When you have finished, turn the unstuffed bear furry side out.

GET STUFFED

Now fill your ted by pushing the stuffing into the hole you left in his back. Use lots of stuffing for a firmer bear and less for a more squashy one. Use a pencil to poke the stuffing into any awkward nooks and crannies like the arms and legs. Sew up the hole in the back.

Sew on two buttons for eyes if your bear doesn't have them already.

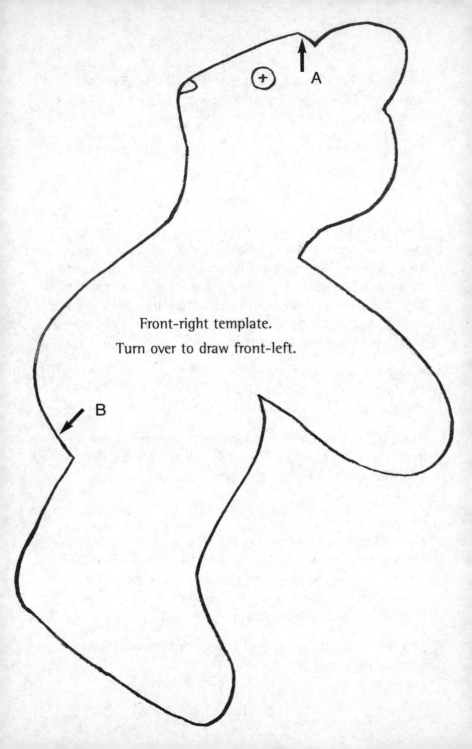

Front-right template.
Turn over to draw front-left.

A

B

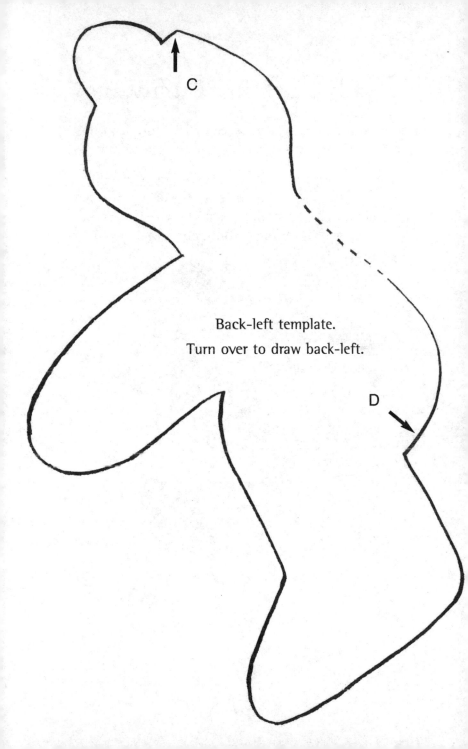

Back-left template.

Turn over to draw back-left.

Funk Up Your Furniture

Breathe new life into a tired piece of furniture with this beautiful craft that dates back to the twelfth century.

The name 'decoupage' comes from the French word 'découper', which means to cut out. By cutting out, then pasting pictures on a wardrobe, chair or chest of drawers, you can give your furniture a stunning finish.

You will need:

- an item of furniture – e.g. chest of drawers, chair, table, lamp stand or wardrobe
- pictures for your design – you can use wrapping paper, wallpaper, posters or magazine pictures
- decoupage medium – a special glue found in any craft store – or PVA glue
- emulsion paint – in a colour that complements the pictures, e.g. a shade of green if you are using floral or leaf designs • sandpaper
- a small roller – from a DIY shop or craft shop
- a small paint brush • a craft knife or scissors
- thick card or cutting board

Let your imagination run riot for a few minutes as you plan you decoupage design. Sketch out a few possible patterns on a piece of paper before picking your favourite. Your pictures can stand alone or overlap if you wish.

Before you start, make sure you put thick card or a cutting board underneath the pictures to protect the surface below. Cut around the outlines of the images with the craft knife or scissors.

Sand down your furniture, removing any dust with a damp cloth. Now apply a thin coat of emulsion paint to the furniture and wait for it to dry.

Arrange your cut-out pictures on a table to make up your

chosen design. Take the paintbrush and coat the back of each image with your decoupage medium or glue. Then paint a thin layer of glue on the area you wish to stick the pictures.

Place the pictures on the furniture, using your fingers to gently smooth down the paper and push out any wrinkles. Run the roller over the cut-outs to ensure any bubbles or wrinkles disappear.

Continue adding new pictures and smoothing them out until they are all in place. Now leave the pictures to dry.

When you are certain everything is thoroughly dry, coat the whole piece of furniture with your decoupage medium or PVA glue, diluted by one part of water to three parts glue, or according to the medium's instructions.

Add more decoupage medium, diluted glue or a clear varnish until the edges of the pictures are smooth. Allow the coating to dry.

Find the perfect spot for your newly revamped furniture. Make sure its eye-catching decoration can be seen from as many angles as possible!

Top tip: Why not pick a bargain piece of furniture from a car-boot sale, then use decoupage to turn it into a treasured family possession?

Meet Mr Turf Top

Give an old pair of Mum's tights a terrific turf toupée with this fun gardening project that'll keep everyone amused for weeks on end.

You will need:

- old nylon tights
- sawdust • grass seed
- elastic bands • a small saucer
- lips cut from felt or fabric
- eyes made from card or wiggle eyes (available in craft shops) • a pair of scissors

Cut off one leg of the tights and discard the rest. Pour a large spoonful of grass seed into the foot and spread it around the toe area. Stuff the end of the tights with sawdust until the 'head' is the size you want.

Secure at the bottom with an elastic band, or simply tie it in a knot. Make sure that the seed is spread evenly where you want the hair to grow. Then create a nose by pinching a small section of nylon and sawdust and wrapping an elastic band around each one. Glue on eyes and lips.

Lastly, soak Mr Turf Top in a small bowl of water so that the sawdust is damp, then sit him comfortably in the saucer and watch his hair grow.

Don't forget to keep the saucer topped up with a little water every so often and give him an occasional trim.

Fresh Pasta Feast

This recipe makes delicious fresh tagliatelle for four people –
perfect to serve up with Mama's Meatballs (See page 152).

You will need:

• 200 g (7 oz) plain flour • 2 eggs • a pinch of salt

Combine the flour and salt in a large bowl. Crack the eggs
into another bowl and beat lightly with a fork. Make a well
in the middle of the flour and pour in the beaten eggs. Stir
together until firm. At this stage, if your dough feels dry,
add a little water – if it seems sticky, add some extra flour.

Place the dough onto a, floured surface and kneed
thoroughly for 10 minutes until smooth and shiny.
Cover in plastic wrap and leave to rest for 15 minutes.

Unwrap the dough and roll it out on a floured surface into
a long rectangle shape about 1 mm thick. Dust the pasta
sheet with flour to prevent sticking and carefully fold the
narrow edge of the sheet over by 4 cm. Continue folding
until the whole sheet is rolled up into a long tube.

Take a knife and cut strips of pasta 1 cm wide from
the folded piece until you reach the end. Unfold the
strips and leave todry for a few minutes before cooking.

Cook the pasta in boiling water for 4 to 5 minutes,
tasting a piece to see if it is ready. Drain and serve.

Mama's Meatballs

This has long been a staple dish in parts of southern Italy and, as many Italian-Americans hail from this region, it has become a firm family-favourite in the US, too.

You will need:

- 2 slices of white bread
- 100 g (4 oz) parmesan cheese, grated
- 400 g (14 oz) lean minced beef
- 1 tbsp fresh parsley, chopped • 2 eggs
- 1 tbsp olive oil • 1 onion, finely chopped
- 2 x 400 g (14 oz) cans chopped tomatoes
- salt and pepper • 400 g (14 oz) dried spaghetti

This recipe will feed four to five hungry people.

Using a food processor, whizz the bread into fine crumbs. If you don't have a food processor, break the bread into crumbs in a bowl. Add the parsley and half of the parmesan cheese and stir together. Add the mince and a good grind of freshly milled black pepper.

Break the eggs into the bowl and mix. Squash the mixture together with your hands until throughly blended.

Roll the mixture into balls the size of a large walnut and place on a baking tray covered in plastic wrap. Put to one side.

Heat the olive oil in a large saucepan and fry the onion until soft. Add the tomatoes and some salt and pepper. Bring to the boil and then turn down the heat to simmer for ten minutes. Drop in the meatballs one by one and then cover the pan. Simmer for one hour.

After about 40 minutes cook the spaghetti according to the instructions on the pack or cook your fresh tagliatelle (see page 151). Drain the pasta and turn into a serving dish. Stir in the cooked meatballs and remaining cheese. Serve immediately.

Top tip: If you prefer a sweeter sauce, add a ½ tsp of sugar to your sauce before you add the meatballs.

Haircare At Home

AVOCADO HAIR PACK

Avocados are packed with vitamins and can give your hair a real treat, rehydrating and leaving it smooth and shiny.

You will need:

- 1 small jar of mayonnaise (not the low-fat type!)
- ½ a ripe avocado • shower cap or plastic wrap

Put the ingredients into a bowl and, using your hands or a spoon, squash the avocado into the mayonnaise until it forms a green paste.

Smooth over the hair, from the roots to the tips. Put on a shower cap (the ones they give you at hotels are ideal for this) or wrap the hair in plastic wrap.

For hair in need of extra deep conditioning, wrap a hot, damp towel over the top of the cap or wrap. This may need two pairs of hands.

Wait for 20 minutes before rinsing with lots of clean, warm water.

LAVENDER HAIR RINSE

This not only smells lovely, but lavender is thought to be a natural remedy for dandruff. Pour half a cup of dried lavender into a pan, with two cups of water. Bring to the boil and simmer for 3 minutes then allow the mixture to cool. Use the lavender water as a hair rinse after washing your hair and leave it on for 15 minutes before rinsing off with water.

ROSEMARY RINSE

Boil a large saucepan of water, then take a bunch of fresh rosemary and add it to the pan. Simmer for half an hour and leave to cool before straining.

This should only be used on dark hair as it can darken blonde hair. It adds shine, helps itchy scalps, and smells really great.

Build A Pixie House

Everyone who believes in elves and pixies knows that they can't resist visiting a garden or park when there's a secret house waiting. Make a hideaway for tiny folk using a handful of natural materials and a sprinkling of imagination.

You will need:

- a small bundle of sticks about 15 cm long
- some string, ribbon or grass • a thimble or acorn shell
- soft moss • feathers or flower heads • small stones

Find a secluded spot in your garden or a nearby park. You will need a small area measuring about 15 cm by 15 cm, away from noisy footsteps. The foot of a tree or behind a bush is perfect, as this will provide your fairy folk with some welcome privacy.

Ideally your chosen spot will have moist soil. This will make your house easier to build. If the soil is dry and hard try sprinkling some water over it.

Collect a small bundle of sticks that are about 15 cm long. Snap longer twigs to this size if necessary, but be sure not to break any twigs or branches off living trees.

Push the sticks about 2 cm into the ground to form a circle shape about 15 cm in diameter. The sticks should point inwards slightly so that they form a cone-shape, like a tepee. Leave a gap in the circle about 4 cm wide for the door, so pixies can tiptoe inside.

Tie the string or ribbon around the top of the twigs to bind them tightly together. It will be easier if one of you holds the twigs together while the other ties them.

Use blades of grass to tie feathers or flowers around the top of the house to make it look more welcoming. Carpet the floor with a layer of luxurious soft moss and place a ring of stones around the edge of the house to protect it from nosy animals. Build a path of stepping-stones leading up to the house using small stones or pebbles to lead the pixies to the door.

Finally, place a thimble, or an acorn shell filled with water, inside the house to welcome thirsty travellers.

Elves and pixies are very shy and so won't use the house until you are well out of the way.

The 'If You Really Had To Choose' Game

This is a great game that can be played anywhere and that should spark some very interesting and bizarre conversations.

Each player takes it in turns to present the other players with an imaginary scenario. The scenario has two possible outcomes, which players have to choose between. The answers 'neither' or 'both' are not allowed.

The scenarios can be as crazy and unrealistic as you like – the quirkier, the better.

For example:

If you really had to choose, one of these animals as a pet, would you rather have a man-eating tiger or a crocodile?

If you really had to choose, would you prefer your left arm to be made from jelly or from cake?

It you really had to choose, would you rather sit in a bath filled with maggots or eat worms?

This game works best if you make your options really difficult to choose between. They could be really yucky, really yummy, really scary, or really funny. This is a fantastic way to find out more about each other, and there are no winners or losers. So what are you waiting for? Get those brain-boggling questions at the ready!

ALSO AVAILABLE:

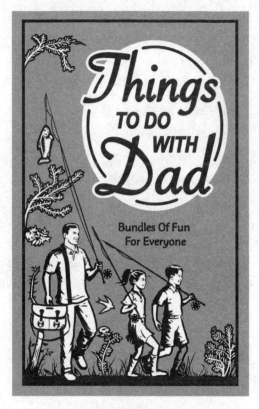

THINGS TO DO WITH DAD
ISBN: 978-1-906082-20-8

If you would like to order this book please contact:

Bookpost, PO Box 29, Douglas, Isle of Man, IM99 1BQ
Tel 01624 677237 Fax 01624 670923